Sasanian Iran
(224–651 CE)

Sasanika Series, No. 1

Published under the auspices of
Dr. Samuel M. Jordan Center for Persian Studies and Culture
University of California, Irvine

About the Series

The purpose of Sasanika Series is to publish scholarly works related to Sasanian civilization in the fields of history, philology, literature, art and archaeology.

Sasanian Iran
(224–651 CE)

Portrait of a Late Antique Empire

Touraj Daryaee

MAZDA PUBLISHERS, Inc. ◆ Costa Mesa, California ◆ 2008

Mazda Publishers, Inc.
Academic publishers since 1980
P.O. Box 2603, Costa Mesa, California 92628 U.S.A.
www.mazdapub.com
A. K. Jabbari, Publisher

Library of Congress Cataloging-in-Publication Data
Daryaee,Touraj
Sasanian Iran, 224- 651 CE : Portrait of a Late Antique Empire/
by Touraj Daryaee.
p. cm.—(Sasanika series ; no. 1)
Includes bibliographical references and index.
ISBN: 1-56859-169-1
ISBN 13: 978-1-56859-169-8 (alk. paper)
1. Sassanids. 2. Iran—History—To 640.
I. Title.
DS286.D373 2008
939'.405—dc22
2008023074

Credits for the maps and illustrations:
Regards sur la Perse antique, Amis de la Bibliothèque municipale du Blanc et Musée d'Argentomagus, Le Blanc, Saint-Marcel, 1998.
G. Rawlinson, *The Seventh Great Oriental Monarchy*, New York, 1882.
Christine Kondoleon, Editor. *Antioch, The Lost Ancient City*, Princeton University Press and Worcester Art Museum, 2001.

The author and the Dr. Samuel M. Jordan Center for Persian Studies and Culture would like to thank Mrs. Nastaran Akhavan for her financial support in publication of this book, made in memory of Jafar Akhavan.

For my teacher
Michael G. Morony

CONTENTS

List of Maps:

List of Illustrations:

Prolegomena

Ancient Iran in the Context of World History

By almost all measures, the impact of Iran and its civilization on world history has been immense. Often, due to the ever presence of a Eurocentric approach to ancient history, ancient civilizations - besides those of Greece and Rome - have been less studied and their impact either completely dismissed or seriously underestimated. In particular, Egypt, Mesopotamia and Iran, collectively known in the West as the ancient Near Eastern and African Civilizations, are seldom studied in the academic institutions and history departments of the universities in North America and Europe. These "other" civilizations are by and large glossed over in classes, even though their importance is stated, and are then relegated to the departments of Near Eastern Languages and Cultures or Civilizations. This division has brought about interesting consequences for the study of history of antiquity.[1] The first and foremost implication is the treatment of non Greco-Roman people as "people without history," as if only Greeks and Romans had a viable history in antiquity.[2] This view of the past further divides and impairs the study of ancient history as

---

[1] The best historiography of the development of Classical Studies in the past three centuries is by M. Bernal, *The Black Athena. The Afro-asiatic Roots of Classical Civilization*, New Brunswick, N.J., 1987, where he alleges that a preference was given to the "Aryan Model" in place of the "Ancient Model" because of what he calls Europe's "Hellenomania."

[2] The term "people without history," is of course a borrowing from the important work of E. Wolf, *Europe and the People Without History*, Berkeley and Los Angeles, 1982.

a unit and blurs the historical reality of the past. It also hinders the understanding of Greek and Roman history. As J. Wiesehöfer, one of the most eminent ancient Iranian historians has rightly stated: "the Near East must be an integral part of a history of Antiquity, that the civilizations of Greece and the Imperium Romanum become truly comprehensible only when seen within a much larger environment."[3] Despite this, through a Eurocentric division, qualitative hierarchies have been attached to civilizations and regions, assigning each section of Eurasian history its own isolated historians and a segregated place in the academic settings in the West.

Fernand Braudel once stated that "Europe invented historians and then made good use of them."[4] This "good use," I contend, is the promotion of one vision of ancient history and civilization - namely those that the modern Europeans and Americans wish to associate themselves with, specifically Greece and Rome – and forsaking those civilizations[5] that were certainly older and as significant in the formation of our common civilization today as Greece and Rome.

This is not to demote the importance of the Greek and Roman civilization, rather to caution the reader that by

---

[3] J. Wiesehöfer, *Iraniens, Grecs et Romains*, Studia Iranica, Cahier 32, Paris, 2005, p. 47. He has also discussed this matter in another important article on the issue of the place and position of the Sasanian Empire in ancient history, "Statt einer Einleitung: 'Randkultur' oder 'Nabel der Welt'? Das Sasanidenreich und der Westen. Anmerkungen eines Althistorikers," *Ērān ud Anērān. Studien zu den Beziehungen zwischen dem Sasanidenreich und der Mittelmeerwelt. Beiträge des Internationalen Colloquiums in Eutin, 8.-9. Juni 2000*, eds. J. Wiesehöfer and Ph. Huyse, München, 2006, pp. 9-28.

[4] F. Braudel, *The Perspective of the World: Civilization and Capitalism 15th-18th Century*, University of California Press, Berkeley & Los Angeles, 1992, p. 134.

[5] S. Amin, *Eurocentrism*, New York, 1989, pp. 93-94.

privileging one region and forsaking the others, modern historical scholarship has succeeded in presenting a lopsided view of the past predicated on the "success" of modern European society and its overseas extensions. This success, simplistically thought to be eternal, is in fact only a temporary economic and specifically industrial dominance determined by four centuries of colonialism and two hundred years of Industrial Revolution, often coinciding with the economic decline of the regions more traditionally dominant in *longue durée* world history and at their cost and progressive underdevelopment. Presently, while Europe and the United States have reached this economic and political hegemony, many of its historians have attempted to manipulate the past and somehow make a case for the uniqueness of the (Western) European civilization and its self-designated "exclusive" ancestors, the Greco-Romans.[6]

As one of the underprivileged histories, the study of ancient Iranian history faces several obstacles, not entirely the fault of the Eurocentric view of ancient history, nor the predicament of the New World Order. The first and foremost is the disparate and multi-lingual nature of the sources which exist for ancient Iranian history. Almost as important is the geographical expanse of this civilization, consisting of the Iranian Plateau and its neighboring lowlands. The first Persian Empire, the Achaemenids (550-330 BCE) which stretched from the "Danube to the Indus"[7] in its largest extent, did not privilege Old Persian as the language of its multi-ethnic and multi-lingual empire. Rather

---

[6] For a successful critique of this view see J.M. Blaut, *The Colonizers' Model of the World*: Geographical Diffusionism and Eurocentric History, Trenton, N.J., 1993.

[7] P. Briant, "Du Danube à l'Indus, l'histoire d'un empire," *L'Iran et la Perse, Le Monde de la bible*, No. 106, 1997, p. 23.

those languages that best created the environment for managing this huge empire, namely Elamite and Aramaic, were given momentum. In the Sasanian Empire we also face a similar trend. While Middle Persian was the official language of the Sasanian dynasty, Sogdian, Bactrian and other languages were also commonly used. With the Muslim conquest, some of the texts were lost, but many others were translated into Arabic as it was mandated by the Muslims that one language is to be used as the *lingua franca* of the early Islamicate world. Indeed this was a very different mental view of language and power than that of late antiquity and the Sasanian order of things.

The second problem is that there are only a few historians who study ancient Iran, and I do not mean dealing with this civilization when it only comes face to face with Greece or Rome, although that has its benefits for the field as well. Indeed, one can easily count the entire body of historians dealing with ancient Iran from memory. If indeed, as it is often alleged, there are no positions in the history departments, then why is ancient Iranian history offered as a field at all? This is a vicious circle that could change by support from outside institutions, governments and individuals, but most importantly by the entire field of history adopting a global and broader perspective.

The third problem has to do with the fact that ancient Iranian history has relied heavily on philology. This means the history of ancient Iran is tangled in the linguistic and philological niceties and rarely given a historical treatment, using methods and approaches designed for history. In this sense, ancient Iranian history has become the domain of Iranian philologists and archaeologists, although the Islamic history of Iran has been far better off. This fact has made ancient Iranian history a fetish of some sorts, seemingly mysterious and far from the reach of most historians. Now historians have made attempts at reclaiming the history of ancient Iran and making it a matter for those well exercised in the historical approach to ancient times. I myself have very much tried to engage in the study of ancient Iranian history in dialogue with the historians of Rome, India, Asia and Caucasus, as well as those working on the economic, cultural and social history of the world or those interested in the roots and precedents of Islamic history and late antiquity. It is only in this way that ancient Iranian history can be released from philology and archaeology, and at the same time take advantage of the sources of knowledge brought about by these fields.

So, it might be appropriate to preface this book by asking who the Iranian People are. The early Iranian people were a population who spoke languages classified as a branch of Indo-European by the linguists. Some of these languages were used for inscriptions and texts and others for oral communication. They include Avestan, Median, Persian, Scythian, Parthian, Sogdian and other smaller groups who moved to the Iranian Plateau in waves, first to Central Asia and modern day Turkemenistan and then to the plateau itself. Three of them, the Medes, the Arsacids and the Persians established kingdoms and empires or centers of power in antiquity. Medes were the first group to be able to consolidate power on the Iranian Plateau and conquer northern Mesopotamia and parts of Anatolia in the seventh century BCE, often at the expense of the Assyrians. This was the beginning of a process by which the land mass between the Mediterranean Sea and the Persian Gulf was united, where trade could pass from the Indian subcontinent to the Mediterranean world. The Achaemenid Persian Empire in 550 BCE, under the leadership of one of the most brilliant political and military leaders, a Persian named Cyrus the Great, was able to reconstitute the Median Kingdom and add all of Mesopotamia to it. By the time of the reign of its third ruler, Darius the Great, the three great river civilizations of antiquity, namely the Nile Basin, Mesopotamia and the Indus Plain, were united under the same political power. For the first time in history an empire was formed which stretched from the Indus to the Nile, with a network of roads, centralized monetary system and a provincial organization, headed by a massive operating bureaucracy.

With Alexander the Great, Iran maintained its importance and stability. I very much subscribe to the views of the great Achaemenid historian, Pierre Briant, where he sees Alexander as the continuation and culmination of the Achaemenid Persian rule.[8] With Alexander's passing, the third ancient Iranian dynasty, the Seleucids, came to power. There are two ways of looking at the Seleucid Empire in the third century BCE. One is to conceive the Seleucids as imperialists who, like their western European successors some eighteen centuries later, came and established their colonial rule in Asia. The other view is that the Seleucids, although Greek in origin, were a force that initiated a Greco-Iranian civilization and continued the path of Iranian history. As with the Achaemenids, we must remember that it is not the language that defines an empire, rather its system of thought, aspirations, organization and aims. In this sense, one can easily make a case for the Seleucids being the third ancient Iranian dynasty. With the weakening of the Seleucid rule over Iran, the fourth dynasty, that of the Arsacids, rose to power. This time from the northeastern fringes of the empire, an Iranian people were able to establish a relatively centralized system which

---

[8] The title of his monumental book, *From Cyrus to Alexander. A History of the Persian Empire*, Eisenbrauns, 2002 points to the same fact, but also see his conclusions, pp. 873-876.

lasted for almost five centuries (247 BCE – 224 CE). The Arsacids were able to amalgamate the Greco-Iranian tradition and to allow different people - be it Greek or Iranian, with different religious affiliation - live side by side.

The religion associated with the Iranian world is of course Zoroastrianism, which manifests itself in various forms. However, one aspect of it, what we may call the Mazdean or Mazdyasnan ("Mazda-worshiping") tradition, i.e. devotion to the supreme deity Ahura Mazda / Ohrmazd remained constant. Still there were other vibrant religions which the Iranian people gravitated towards. From the Achaemenid period onwards, Jews had lived in Iran and cooperated with the Persian administration, whether in Ecbatana/Hamedan, Babylonia or Jerusalem. Under the Arsacids, Jewish Persian officers served in the army and the regular propaganda assigned the Iranian dynasty a role as saviors, while the Romans were seen as the oppressors. Christianity also found safety from Roman persecution in the Iranian realms, starting in the first century CE. It was only in the third and the fourth centuries that Christianity was held under suspicion, but by the fifth century Persian Christianity itself was recognized by the Sasanian kings and the state. Buddhism and to a far lesser extent Hinduism found a foothold on the eastern fringes of the Iranian World. The Buddhas of Bamiyan are a testament to the vibrant Buddhist community in the eastern Iranian world. We should also mention the Mandeans who lived in Mesopotamia and live there till today, as well as Manichaeans whose religious ideas were almost adopted by a Sasanian monarch in the third century CE.

The fifth ancient Iranian dynasty is the Sasanian Empire whose political history is the subject of this book. The Sasanians are instrumental in the formation of the idea of Iran as a nation and its belief system, moral and ethical values and the language and literature of the Persianate World. It was the Sasanians who forged the concept of a territorial boundary called Ērānšahr or "realm of the Iranians," which in a secularized form, passed on even after the fall of the Sasanians themselves.

The same idea was regularly invoked by the Samanid, Ghaznavid, Mongol, Safavid, Qajar and the Pahlavi dynasties and survives to our day. This traditional historical horizon of the Iranians is encapsulated in the great Persian epic of Šāhnāmeh, the "Book of Kings," which was originally composed as the royal chronicle, the Xwadāy-nāmag "Book of Lords," in the Sasanian period. Zoroastrianism as we know it today would not have been established were it not for the Zoroastrian priests in the Sasanian period who committed the Avesta and its twenty one nasks "chapters" - the sacred hymns of that tradition - to writing. It was the Sasanians who firmly established a Persian tradition, with a society based on communal religions in a place called Ērānšahr or Ērān / Iran. When the Sasanians fell to the Arab Muslims, the tradition was so strong that it also influenced Islam and the Persian culture without subsiding. Since the late Qajar and the early Pahlavi period, it has been normal to think of the fall of the Sasanian Empire to the Muslims as the end of all that was glorious and indeed as the demise of Iran. But cultures do not die, or at least Persian culture did not die and as what it had done with Hellenism, now it did with Islam. Under Islam, the Iranian culture managed to be the driving force in the cultural, artistic, intellectual and literary aspects of the Islamic world. This indeed is the genius of Iranian civilization in that it has been able to absorb foreign conquests and invading cultures into its own tradition and create a universal tradition in return.

This short book attempts to present an outline of the history of Sasanian Iran (224-651 CE) based on the most recent studies. The study of Sasanian history is very much a neglected field, so much so that when I wrote a first draft of this book several years ago for the Sasanika Project (www.sasanika.com) I was contacted from near and far for permission to cite by the scholars of other periods of Iranian history or other civilizations of the same time period.

It is baffling to me that this piece should merit such reaction, but this reaction goes to show that we are in a dire need of much more in depth study of Sasanian Iran and its history. One can easily survey the existing books on Sasanian history and civilization. The two parts of volume three of *The Cambridge History of Iran*, edited by Ehsan Yarshater not only deal with the Sasanians, but also with the Arsacids. Richard Nelson Frye's two important books, the *Heritage of Persia*, and *The History of Ancient Iran* deal with the entire period of ancient Persian / Iranian history, where the Sasanians are covered in a chapter or two. Most recently, J. Wiesehöfer's excellent book, *Ancient Persia* has provided a complete survey of ancient Iranian history, including the Sasanian period. Consequently, those who want to find a specific book on Sasanian Iran are forced to consult either the classic work of Arthur Christensen, *L'Iran sous les Sassanides,* written in 1944 in French or Klaus Schippmann's *Grundzüge der Geschichte des sasanidischen Reiches* written in 1990 in German. Then it is not surprising that a relatively short piece in English from the internet as part of my Sasanika Project should receive such attention. Of course this is not to forget the contributions of the scholars who have done much in the past two or three decades to help our understanding of the Sasanian history and civilization. Ph. Gignoux and R. Gyselen in France have revolutionized the epigraphic and administrative history of the Sasanian Empire. M. Alram along with other numismatists such as V. Sarkhosh Curtis, M.I. Mochiri, H.M. Malek, A. Gariboldi and others have given us new ways of understanding political, religious and administrative history. Sh. Shaked, G. Gnoli, A. de Jong, M. Stausberg and others have given us a fresh look at religion in the Sasanian period. The linguistic and philological works of P. O. Skjærvø, A. Panaino, C.G. Cereti, M. Macuch and Ph. Huyse have provided better versions of Middle Iranian texts. Finally, Z. Rubin and J. Wiesehöfer, among others, have tried to make Sasanian history matter in the field of ancient history.

Based on the work of all these scholars in the past decades, I have assumed that a printed version of the internet text with additional observations merits a publication in the Sasanika series under the auspices of the Dr. Samuel M. Jordan Center for Persian Studies and Culture at the University of California, Irvine and Mazda Publishers. I wish to thank Dr. A. Kamron Jabbari for agreeing to undertake the publication of the Sasanika series and to make it see the light of day. I also would like to thank another student of Sasanian history, Khodadad Rezakhani, for reading a draft of this book and making substantial comments and corrections. Without his help this text would not see the light of day. The shortcomings are of course mine alone.

Finally, I would like to dedicate this book to someone who has made me who I am as a scholar. I am a historian and am trained in the history department at the University of California, Los Angeles. My teacher, M.G. Morony, himself has toiled to demonstrate the importance of Sasanian history, not only for late antiquity but also for the post-Sasanian / Islamic period in a time when there was hardly any attention paid to this period of Near Eastern history.

Near Eastern history in the West has commonly begun with the Sumerians and end with Alexander. It then begins again with the Arab Muslims and the Islamic history. The gap in between has been the purview of Greco-Roman historians. Morony has tried to change this nebulous view of Near Eastern history. In a sense, he has opened the Pandora's Box and trained and encouraged most people who deal with Sasanian history today in the United States. He should be thanked and honored for this work and as such, I would like to dedicate this book to him.

Touraj Daryaee
Howard Baskerville Professor in the History of Iran and the Persianate World
University of California, Irvine

I

Iran before the Sasanians

The Iranian Plateau has been the home of many important civilizations. Haltamti or Elam stands as the first major civilization which has left an abundant literary and material culture, from the fourth millennium BCE to the first millennium BCE. Elam was one of the first civilizations in the world to create systems of calculation and writing.[1] In turn, Achaemenid Persians who were deeply influenced by the world of Elam created the first true world empire. As already mentioned, the foremost historian of the Achaemenid world, P. Briant has called the geographical expanse of the Achaemenid Persians "from the Danube to the Indus." This dominance unified many regions of Eurasia for the first time in history. The interaction then pulled various religious, technological and political ideas together and brought the known world into a new phase of its existence under the Persian rule. This interaction took place in an atmosphere of tolerance which the world had rarely witnessed.

---

[1] For a treatment of calculation and writing system which developed in Iran see chapter II of C. Herrenschmidt, *Les Trios écritures: Langue, nombre, code*, Gallimard, 2007.

In the fourth century BCE, Alexander the Great was able to conquer the Satrapies of the Persian empire. Even in this Greco-Macedonian venture one can see Alexander not as a foreign conqueror, but as one who attempted to justify his conquest by claiming to be the rightful successor to the Persian throne. As his conquests took him to the heart of the Achaemenid lands, he began to adopt Persian customs, partake in the ceremonies of the Magi and marry Iranian princesses to continue the royal Achaemenid line. For Persia, to follow P. Briant's view again, Alexander was only the last of the Achaemenid rulers.[2] The Greco-Macedonians became part of an already existing world order whose mastery they had just acquired.

The Seleucids, successors to Alexander, established themselves in the former Achaemenid territories and ruled from 312 to 208 BCE. This dynasty only nominally controlled the Iranian Plateau and by 250 BCE, it already showed signs of weakness and fragmentation. Other Greco-Macedonian colonies had been established on the Iranian Plateau, but many institutions were those of the former Persian empire.[3]

Around 238 BCE, the Arsacids had invaded the eastern Iranian Plateau and a new dynasty, mindful of both its Iranian and Greco-Macedonian heritage was established. The Arsacids in time gravitated more and more towards the Iranian culture and adopted the ideas and ideals of the

---

[2] P. Briant, "The Seleucid Kingdom, the Achaemenid Empire and the History of the Near East in the First Millennium BC," *Religion and Religious Practice in the Seleucid Kingdom*, Aarhus, 1990, pp. 44.

[3] The best books for studying Seleucid history in the context of Iranian and Near Eastern history are A. Kuhrt and S. Sherwin-White, *From Samarkhand to Sardis: A New Approach to the Seleucid Empire*, London, 1993, and most recently, L. Capdetrey, *Le pouvoir séleucide: Territoire, administration, finances d'un royaume hellénistique (312-129 avant J.-C.)*, Presses Universitaires de Rennes, 2007.

Achaemenids. While the fortunes of the Arsacids fluctuated, the Persians in Persis acknowledged the king of kings, but also remembered their glorious past. The pre-Sasanian graffiti left at the Persepolis and the continued association of the local Persian rulers with this palace and their building activities suggests this fact. In time, the family of Sāsān, local Persian aristocrats, managed to create another vibrant Persian empire whose borders stretched from the Oxus River and India to Syria and the Arabian Peninsula. How then did the Sasanian Persians establish themselves and what was their importance for the political history of Iran?

Before dealing with the Sasanians we need to look at the political and cultural situation in the province of Persis / Fārs before the rise of the Sasanian dynasty. Following is an inscription that can lead us to the study of the Sasanian political history:

> *ardaxšahr šāh brādā-y-in dārāyānagān pus dārāyān šāh šād hānd ēn YNGDWN zarr asēm 50 statēr wahīxšahr wispuhr xwēbaš*

> "May I give happiness to King Ardaxšahr, our brother, a descendant of Dārāyān, son of King Dārāyān. This hammered (bowl in) gold-and-silver (weighs) 50 staters. (It) belongs to Prince Wahīxšahr."

P.O. Skjærvø who studied this inscription, carved on a silver cup, has made some important observations about the pre-Sasanian dynasts of the province of Persis.[4] He suggests that based on the script used, the cup may be dated to the time of the independent rulers of Persis before

---

[4] P.O. Skjærvø, "The Joy of the Cup: A Pre-Sasanian Middle Persian Inscription on a Silver Bowl," *Bulletin of the Asia Institute*, vol. 11, 1997, pp. 93-104.

the beginning of the common-era. It appears that Dārā(yān) II made substantial changes not only in linguistic matters, but also set new religious measures, indicated by the iconography. Consequently the period of his rule survived in the historical memory of the Persians of the Sasanian period as the time of the rule of *Dārāy ī Dārāyān.*[5]

Before this Dārā(yān) II, there are a series of rulers in Persis who are known as the *Fratarakā*, which means approximately a "governor" or "superior."[6]   These rulers, whose coinage is our main source, include Baydād, Ardaxšahr / Ardaxšīr I, Wahbarz, Wādfradād I, and Wādfradād II.[7] The important work of J. Wiesehöfer has shed light on this dark period of Persian history and has given us a perspective into the relations between these kings and their Seleucid and the Arsacid overlords.

Coin of Wahbarz

On the coin of Wahbarz, for example, we find the legend *whwbrz prtrk' zy 'lhy' br prs* "Wahbarz, governor of the gods, son of a Persian." The importance of this legend lies

---

[5] *Ibid.*, p. 103.

[6] For a review of literature on the *fratarakā* see Wiesehöfer, *Die "Dunklen Jahrhunderte" der Persis. Untersuchungen zur Geschichte und Kultur von Fārs in frühhellenistischer Zeit (330-140 v. Chr.)*, Munich, 1994, pp. 105-108; also his "Fars under Seleucid and Parthian Rule," *The Idea of Iran, The Age of the Parthians*, eds. V. Sarkhosh Curtis and S. Stewart, vol. 2, London, 2007, pp. 37-49.

[7] For the list of kings see J. Wiesehöfer, 1994, p. 114.

in the fact that the early Sasanian legend *MNW ctry MN yzd'n / kē čihr az yazdān* "from the race of gods" might be reminiscent of this Fratarakā's title. This is significant in that it might suggest that the Persians were susceptible to the Seleucid propaganda and were not so reactionary to Hellenism. In fact the Fratarakā supported the Seleucids, even when the Arsacids stepped onto the Iranian Plateau.[8] It is for the very same reason that when the Arsacids came to power, they also adopted the existing titles, including Θεοπάτωρ, "of divine descent."[9]

The next group of coinage begins with Dārā(yān) and is followed by Wādfradād, Dārā(yān) II, Ardaxšahr / Ardaxšīr, Wahuxšahr, Wādfradād, Manūčihr, Ardaxšahr / Ardaxšīr, Manūčihr, and Nāmbad who took the title of king *MLKA / šāh*.[10]

---

[8] Wiesehöfer, 1994, pp. 105-108; *ibid.,* "Fārs II. – History in the Pre-Islamic Period," *Encycelopaedia Iranica,* ed. E. Yarshater, vol. IX, New York, 1999, p. 335.

[9] A. Gariboldi, "Royal and Ideological Patterns Between Seleucid and Parthian Coins: The Case of Θεοπάτωρ," in *Commerce and Monetary Systems in the Ancient World: Means of Transmission and Cultural Interaction, Melammu Symposia V,* ed. R. Rollinger and Ch. Ulf with collaboration of K. Schnegg, Franz Steiner Verlag, 2004, pp. 367, 374, 375. For the latest treatment of the Fratarakas and contrary to my supposition see A. Panaino, "The baγān of the Fratarakas: Gods or 'divine' Kings?," *Religious themes and texts of pre-Islamic Iran and Central Asia: Studies in honour of Professor Gherardo Gnoli on the occasion of his 65th birthday on 6 December 2002,* eds. C. Cereti, M. Maggi, E. Provasi, Wiesbaden, 2002, pp. 283-306; P. Callieri who sees the structure on the reverse of Persis coins as a place of crowning of the local ruler has suggested that the funerary cult and the taking of the title of *baγān* "gods" in fact may represent an attachment to the Achaemenids and against the Hellenistic rule of the Seleucids, "A proposito di un'iconografia monetale dei dinasti del Fārs post-achemenide," *OCNUS,* vol, 6, 1998, p. 36.

[10] R.N. Frye, *The History of Ancient Iran,* München, 1983, p. 272.

Coin of Dārā(yān)

The onomastic and iconographic evidence furnished by these coins imply that a memory of the Achaemenid kings was current and the attachment to the cult of fire which is basic to Zoroastrianism was also present. The fact that the coinage of Ardaxšīr I, the founder of the Sasanian dynasty is similar to these coins should tell us of a vibrant Persian tradition and the attachment of the various local rulers to it.

II

Ardaxšīr I and the Establishment of the Sasanian Empire[1]

[1] The basic outline of Sasanian history is based on al-Tabarī, *Ta'rīkh al-rusul wa-al-mulūk*, ed. M.J. de Goeje, Leiden, 1879-1901. The English translation with copious notation is by C.E. Bosworth, *The History of al-Tabarī, Vol. V, The Sāsānids, the Byzantines, the Lakhmids, and Yemen*, State University of New York Press, 1999; Secondary sources, M. Morony, "Sāsānids," *The Encycleopaedia of Islam*, 1998; A. Christensen, *L'Iran sous les Sassanides*, Copenhagen, 1944; R.N. Frye, *The History of Ancient Iran*, C.H. Beck'sche Verlagsbuchhandlung, München, 1983, pp. 281-340; *ibid.*, "The Political History of Iran Under the Sasanians," *The Cambridge History of Iran*, ed. E. Yarshater, Vol. 3(1), 1983, pp. 116-180; K. Schippmann, *Grundzüge der Geschichte des sasanidischen Reiches*, Darmstadt, 1990; J. Wiesehöfer, *Ancient Persia From 550 BC to 650 AD*, I.B. Tauris Publishers, London & New York, 1996, pp. 151-222; Z. Rubin, "The Sasanid Monarchy," *The Cambridge Ancient History*, vol. 14, 2000, pp. 638-661; For a comprehensive overview and important notices on Sasanian and Roman empire in a comparative perspective see J. Howard-Johnston, "The Two Great Powers in Late Antiquity: a Comparison," *The Byzantine and Early Islamic Near East*, vol. III, ed. A. Cameron, The Darwin Press, Inc., New Jersey, 1995, pp. 157-226; for the Sasanian – Roman relations see B. Dignas and E. Winter, *Rome and Persia in Late Antiquity. Neighbours and Rivals*, Cambridge, 2007. For the map of the Sasanian Empire see E. Kettenhofen, *Das Sāsānidenreich*, TAVO, Dr. Ludwig Reichert Verlag, Wiesbaden, 1993.

pas az marg ī aleksandar ī hrōmīg ērānšahr dō sad ud čehel
kadag-xwadāy būd

"after the death of Alexander the Roman, Ērānšahr
had two hundred and forty feudal lords (petty
kings)."

This passage from the *Kārnāmag ī Ardaxšīr ī Pābagān*
provides us with the Sasanian view of history before their rule.[2] Thus, the unification of the Iranian
Plateau is presented as a monumental task undertaken by
Ardaxšīr ī Pābagān.[3] The origins of the house of Sāsān as
well as that of Ardaxšīr himself are a mystery. There are
many different stories regarding the origins of Ardaxšīr
and his family. One must be aware that an upstart, in order to gain legitimacy, would naturally have claimed descent from the ancients. Ardaxšīr is an excellent example of
a ruler with an ambiguous lineage, as the array of titles
and stories about him suggest.

We know that Ardaxšīr chose Sāsān as the eponymous
ancestor of his dynasty. An ostracon found in eastern Iran
from an earlier period has the epigraphic form *ssn*. Scholars previously believed that this is to be identified with
Sāsān.[4] However, M. Schwartz has now shown that the
name mentioned on the ostracon has nothing to do with
Sāsān, but represents *Sesen*, an old Semitic god which is

---

[2] *Kārnāmag ī Ardaxšīr ī Pābagān*, I.1, F. Grenet, *La Geste d'ardashir fils de pâbag, Kārnāmag ī Ardaxšīr ī* Pābagān, editions A Die, 2003, p. 52.
[3] G. Widengren, "The Establishment of the Sasanian dynasty in the light of new evidence," *La Persia nel Medioevo*, Academia Nazionale dei Lin-cei, Roma, 1971, pp. 711-782; J. Wiesehöfer, "Ardašīr I," *Encyclopaedia Iranica*, ed. E. Yarshater, vol. II, 1987, pp. 371-376.
[4] V.A. Livshits, "New Parthian Documents from South Turkemenistan," *Acta Antiqua Academiae Scientiarum Hungaricae*, vol. 25, 1977, p. 176.

found in Ugrait as early as the second millennium BCE.[5] Be that as it may, in the first century CE, however, in Taxila we find coins with the name of *Sasa* which may be connected with *Sāsān* because the emblem on the coin matches those of coat-of-arms for Šābuhr I.[6] As Ph. Gignoux has suggested, *Sāsān* may very well be a protective deity known in Asia, especially invoked against sorcery. This fact is shown by the existence of a seal which states: *sāsān ham sāsān ī bay ud sāsān pāsbān* "O Sāsān, the same Sāsān who is god and Sāsān the protector."[7] Furthermore it was claimed that Ardaxšīr was (*KAP* IV.19) *ardaxšīr ī kay ī pābagān ī az tōhmag ī sāsān nāf ī dārā šāh* "Ardaxšīr the Kayānid, the son of Pābag, from the race of Sāsān, from the family of King Dārāy." When looking at this line one gets the sense that every possible connection to divinity, royalty and nobility was evoked by Ardaxšīr, which can only mean that he was none of them! The Kayānid dynasty in the *Avesta*, the little understood and probably known Sāsān, and the connection to Dārāy (probably Darius III and Dārā(yān) II) all hint at this falsification of a lineage.

The inscription of Ardaxšīr's son, Šābuhr I does, however, mention that Pābag was the father of Ardaxšīr, but he was neither the only son, nor the eldest. Even here we see an ambitious man who is envisioning an empire from his

---

[5] M. Schwartz, "*Sasm, Sesen, St. Sisinnios, Sesengen Barpharangès, and ... 'Semanglof,'" *Bulletin of the Asia Institute*, vol. 10, 1996, pp. 253-257; *ibid.*, "Sesen: a Durable East Mediterranean God in Iran," *Proceedings of the Third European Conference of Iranian Studies held in Cambridge, 11th to 15th September 1995*, Part 1, Old and Middle Iranian Studies, ed. N. Sims-Williams, Wiesbaden, Dr. Ludwig Reichert Verlag, 1998: pp. 9-13.

[6] Frye, 1983, p. 200.

[7] Ph. Gignoux, "Sāsān ou le dieu protecteur," *Proceedings of the Third European Conference of Iranian Studies*, Part 1: Old and Middle Iranian Studies, ed. N. Sims-Williams, Wiesbaden, pp. 4; *ibid.*, *Man and Cosmos in Ancient Iran*, Roma, 2001, p. 72

holdout in the province of Persis. Later Persian and Arabic sources state that Ardaxšīr was the *argbed* (Castilian) of Dārābgird in eastern Persis when he began his campaign. Where we find the earliest physical evidence for Ardaxšīr, however, is at Ardaxšīr-xwarrah (Fērōz-ābād, also known as Gūr), on the southern fringes of the province of Persis. It is from Ardaxšīr-xwarrah, far away from Istakhr, the stronghold of the kings of Persis, and yet farther away from the Arsacid king of kings, Ardawān, that the Persian warlord begun his campaign of conquest.

Ardaxšīr's campaign may be connected to his first rock-relief which shows him at the head of a small retinue, receiving the diadem of rulership from Ohrmazd. The year for this may be 205-206 CE,[8] when he had his first rock-relief as well. This coincides with the rule of Arsacid Walāxš (192-207 CE) and wars with the Roman emperor Septimius Severus.[9] By 211/212 CE Ardaxšīr had been able to subjugate the local petty rulers of the province of Persis. We may assume that all this time Ardaxšīr-xwarrah served as the launching and hiding place for Ardaxšīr and that the fort on the mountain (present day *Qal'e Dokhtar)* served as his stronghold. By this time he had begun minting coins with the title of *bay šāh ardaxšīr* "(His) majesty king Ardaxšīr," to proclaim his aspirations.[10]

---

[8] R. Altheim-Stiehl, "Das früheste Datum der sasanidischen Geschichte, vermittelt durch die Zeitangabe der mittelpersisch-parthischen Inschrift aus Bīšāpūr," *Archäologische Mitteilungen aus Iran*, vol. 11, 1978, p. 116.

[9] Wiesehöfer, 1987, p. 372.

[10] M. Alram, "The Beginning of Sasanian Coinage," *Bulletin of the Asia Institute*, vol. 13, 1999, p. 68; M. Alram & R. Gyselen, *Sylloge Nummorum Sasanidarum Paris –Berlin Wien*, Band I, Wien, 2003, p. 93; for all the titles as reflected in the material culture as well as texts see Ph. Huyse, "Die sasanidische Königstitulatur: Eine Gegenüberstellung der Quellen," *Ērān ud Anērān. Studien zu den Beziehungen zwischen dem Sasanidenreich und der Mittelmeerwelt. Beiträge des Internationalen Colloquiums in Eutin,*

Coin of Šābuhr and Pābag

Obverse: *bgy šhpwhly MLK'* "(His) Majesty, king Šābuhr"
Reverse: *BRH bgy p'pky MLK'* "son of (His) Majesty, king Pābag."

In our sources Pābag, Ardaxšīr's father, is said to have been the priest of the fire-temple of Anāhīd at the city of Istakhr, a place which might have been a stage for rallying the local Persian warriors who were devoted to the cult of this deity.[11] Pābag's priestly function can also be seen from a graffito at Persepolis.[12] One can also see that the proximity of the graffito of Pābag and the Achaemenid structure suggests that these monuments were important for the Sasanians and that they in effect were attempting to be heirs to those who built the Persepolis palaces.

8.-9. Juni 2000, eds. J. Wiesehöfer and Ph. Huyse, München, 2006, pp. 181-202.

[11] For study on the cult of Anāhīd see M.L. Chaumont, "Le culte de la déesse Anāhitā (Anahit) dans la religion des monarques d'Iran et d'Arménie au Ier siècle de notre ère," *Journal Asiatique*, Vol. 253, 1965, pp. 168-171; and her "Le culte de Anāhitā à Stakhr et les premiers Sassanides," *Revue de l'Histoire des Religions*, Vol. 153, 1958, pp. 154-175. Tabarī also gives further information, *The History of al-Tabarī*, translated by C.E. Bosworth, 1999, p. 4.

[12] E. Herzfeld, *Iran in the Ancient East*, Hacker Art Books, New York, reprint 1988, p. 309; P. Callieri, "At the roots of the Sasanian royal imagery: the Persepolis graffiti," *Ērān ud Anērān: Studies Presented to Boris Il'ič Maršak on the Occasion of His 70th Birthday*, eds. M. Compareti, P. Raffetta, G. Scarcia, Venice, 2006, pp. 129-148.

One should not, however, completely brush away the idea that Pābag was the priest at the Anāhīd fire-temple of Istakhr. It might have well been his religious influence which gave backing to Ardaxšīr's claim to rulership and provided a much needed association with the Zoroastrian tradition. Anāhīd in particular is important, since she is a much praised deity in the Zoroastrian sacred text, the *Avesta*, (see Yašt V, the *Ābān Yašt*), and has heroes, warriors and kings as her devotees. Her warlike character were the symbiosis of ancient Near Eastern (Ištar), Hellenic (Athena / Anaitis) and Iranian traditions which provided legitimation for kingship in the Sasanian period.[13] During the Achaemenid period, at the beginning of the fifth century BCE, Artaxerxes II also worshipped Anāhīd (Anāhīta) along with Mīhr (Mithra) and Ohrmazd (Ahurā Mazdā). Thus her cult was quite established in Persis and the temple might have been a location where the Persian tradition was kept alive. Consequently, Pābag might have presented the doubled priest-king identity which is a recurrent pattern in Iranian dynastic historiography.

Additionally, the official Sasanian historiography states that it was Pābag who dethroned the king of Istakhr, Gozīhr.[14] The question would then be why Ardaxšīr I should claim to be a king if his father Pābag had dethroned the local king at Istakhr? This issue may hint at tensions between Pābag and Ardaxšīr's aspirations for their family and the issue of succession to the rulership of Persis. It ap-

---

[13] A. Piras, "Mesopotamian Sacred Marriage and Pre-Islamic Iran," *Melammu Symposia IV*, eds. A. Panaino and A. Piras, Milano, 2004, p. 251.

[14] Agathias, *The Histories*, Book 2.27, p. 61. For Pābag and his relationship to Ardaxšīr see R.N. Frye, "Zoroastrian Incest," *Orientalia Iosephi Tucci Memoriae Dicata*, eds. G. Gnoli and L. Lanciotti, Istituto Italiano per il Medio ed Estremo Oriente, Roma, 1985, pp. 445-455; also M. Shaki, "Sasan ke bud?," *Iranshenasi*, vol. 2, no. 1, Spring 1990, pp. 78-80.

pears that Pābag had not chosen Ardaxšīr as the king, but the young man himself aspired to the throne. The early coins of the Sasanians indicate that Pābag had designated his elder son, Šābuhr as the heir.

However, Ardaxšīr apparently was not satisfied with this arrangement and rebelled either against his father or after his father's death against his elder brother Šābuhr. Sasanian historiography tells us that before the two brothers met in battle, Šābuhr died accidentally. Did Ardaxšīr have his brother killed? We will never know for sure, but Ardaxšīr's ambition would have encouraged him to take such a step. Soon (211/212 CE?), he became the king of Persis. It had taken him five years to take control of the province of Persis from his stronghold in Ardaxšīr-Xwarrah.

He then began a struggle against the Arsacid ruler, Ardawān IV. This conflict, which may have lasted a decade, was spent consolidating his power in Persis and expanding his conquests to the adjoining regions, actions which naturally alarmed Ardawān. At the same time, other brothers of Ardaxšīr were also worrying him and he was forced to deal with them.[15] Ardawān, himself was previously challenged by another Arsacid, Walāxš (Vologases VI) who minted coins in his own name until 221-222 CE, demonstrating the fact that the matter of an all powerful "king of kings" had not been settled in the Arsacid empire.[16] It was thus not difficult for a local warrior in the province of Persis to rise and begin conquering the surrounding territories in a short time, away from international and dynastic conflict.

In response to Ardaxšīr's success, Ardawān sent several armies to subjugate him, but each time the young Persian was victorious. The Arsacid king now had to take matters

---

[15] Widengren, pp. 725-726.
[16] Schippmann, p. 70.

into his own hands and once and for all finish the work that his subject kings and generals could not. However, it was finally Ardaxšīr I who was able to defeat Ardawān (Artabanus IV) at the plain of Hormozgān in 224 CE and establish the Sasanian empire.[17] From then on Ardaxšīr took the title of *šāhān šāh* "King of Kings" and began the conquest of a territory which would be called *Ērānšahr* or simply *Ērān* / Iran.

But prior to this fateful battle between the last Arsacid king and Ardaxšīr, much had happened which did not suggest a decline of the Arsacid dynasty. Ardawān had held his own, fighting the emperor Caracalla and the Romans close to Nisibis in 217 CE. A treaty in 218 CE brought a monetary settlement and kept most of Mesopotamia in the hands of the Arsacids. The next two Roman emperors, Elagabalus (218-222 CE) and Alexander Severus (222-235 CE) faced many troubles in the Roman empire, preventing them from making the Arsacids and then the Sasanians their sole priority. Thus, it is amazing that the Arsacid army which was able to confront the Romans, fell to Ardaxšīr and the Persian forces at the plain of Hormozgān.

The battle of Hormozgān

We should say more about Ardaxšīr, since he is an important personage in the development of the Sasanian his-

---

[17] *Dio's Roman History*, Book LXXX.3, 1-2 mentions that Ardaxšīr was victorious in three battle against the Arsacids; Herodian Book VI.2, 6-7.

tory and imperial ideology. The material remains of his rule are especially rich in providing us with his world-view. In commemoration of his victory, he commissioned several rock-reliefs at Naqsh-e Rajab, Naqsh-e Rustam, and at Fērūzābād (Ardaxšīr-Xwarrah). At Naqsh-e Rustam, he is shown on his horse standing over the dead body of Ardawān. Ohrmazd faces him, mounted on a horse, which stands over the body of the evil spirit Ahreman, and is handing the symbol of sovereignty to Ardaxšīr I.[18]

Investiture scene of Ardaxšīr with Ohrmazd at Naqsh-e Rustam

This relief shows that Ardaxšīr believed or wanted others to believe that he was appointed by God to rule over a territory, called *Ērānšahr* in the inscription. The name, which had precedence in the *Avesta* and designated the mythical homeland of the Aryans, was now transposed onto the region where the Sasanians were ruling.[19] This

---

[18] For Ardaxšīr's reliefs showing him at the battle of Hormozgan and other reliefs see W. Hinz, *Altiranische Funde und Forschungen*, Walter de Gruyter & Co., Berlin, 1969, pp. 127-134; G. Herrmann, *The Iranian Revival*, Elsevier, Phaidon, 1977, pp. 87-90.

[19] G. Gnoli, *The Idea of Iran, an Essay on Its Origin*, Serie Orientale Roma LXII, Rome, 1989.

idea was to be accepted by the Zoroastrian and non-Zoroastrian population of the empire and has lived on in the collective memory of Iranians in various stages and strata of the Iranian society till modern times.

This idea should not be mistaken for the Classical historian's testimonies, who believed that Ardaxšīr was attempting to regain the Achaemenid Persian territory.[20] What is clear is that a notion of what Ērānšahr meant was present in the religious sphere, which may have given rise to political concepts of a set territory. This is gained from the third century inscriptions of the Zoroastrian priest Kerdīr who describes what was considered to be Ērānšahr and what was considered to be an-Ērān or non-Iranian. Kerdīr tells us that he established many fires and appointed priests in Ērān, which according to him included the following provinces: Persis, Parthia, Babylonia, Mesene, Adiabene, Azerbaijan, Isfahan, Ray, Kerman, Sistan, and Gurgan, to Peshawar. According to him, Syria, Cilicia, Armenia, Georgia, Albania and Balasgan which were under Sasanian control were deemed as an-Ērān.[21] This term is also used in an adjectival form, giving Ērīh "Iranianess," and an antonym, an-Ērīh along with all its cultural designations.

Ardaxšīr's coins[22] also bear a standard formula which the succeeding kings in the third and the fourth centuries adopted: mazdysn bgy ... MLK'n MLK' 'yl'n MNW ctry MN yzd'n "Mazdaean Majesty, (name of the king), King of

---

[20] Herodian, Book VI.2.2-3.

[21] Ph. Gignoux, Les Quatre inscriptions du mage Kirdīr, textes et concordances, Association pour l'avancement des études iraniennes, Leuven, 1991, p. 71.

[22] Alram, 1999, pp. 67-76.

Kings of *Ērān,* whose lineage / image (is) from the gods."[23] According to this legend, Ardaxšīr considered himself a worshiper of Mazda (Ohrmazd) *"mazdysn"* first and foremost.[24] Secondly, he presented himself as having divine parentage *"MNW ctry MN yzd'n."* This of course brings us to the question of from whom did he believe he was descended? Which "gods" were his forefathers?

Still with this difficulty and confusion, we can state that Ardaxšīr saw himself as the descendent of the gods *"yazdān,"* and the Sasanians may have elevated *Sāsān* to divine status.[25] It is altogether possible that this idea was

---

[23] For Sasanian coins see R. Göbl, *Sasanidische Numismatik,* Klinkhardt & Biermann, Braunschweig, 1968; M. Alram, *Iranische Personennamenbuch, Nomia Propria Iranica in Nummis,* vol. 4, ed. M. Mayrhofer and R. Schmitt, Vienna, 1986.

[24] A. Panaino has emphasized the human character of the Sasanian king and his lack of divine attributes, see "Astral Characters of Kingship in the Sasanian and Byzantine World," *La Persia e Bisanzio,* Accademia Nazionale dei Lincei, Roma, 2004, p. 558.

[25] In Šābuhr's inscription at Ka'be-ye Zardošt (ŠKZ 25/20/46), Sāsān is called: s's'n ZY MR'HY *sāsān ī xwadāy* "Sāsān the Lord." While the Middle Persian word *xwadāy* stands for "lord" in the political sense, there are instances where it also accompanies Ohrmazd, thus giving the word a spiritual sense. For *xwadāy* see M.R. Shayegan, "The Evolution of the Concept of Xwadāy 'God'," *Acta Orientalia Academiae Scientiarum Hungaricae,* Vol. 51, Nos. 1-2, 1998, pp. 31-54. The tradition of deification of the ruler/king that became important with Alexander under Egyptian influence may have influenced the Persians as well. See T. Daryaee, "Laghab-e Pahlavī-ye 'čihr az yazdān' va Šāhanšāhī-ye Sāsānī," *Nāme-ye Farhangestān,* Vol. 4, No. 4, 2000, pp. 28-32; *ibid.,* "Notes on Early Sasanian Titulature," *Journal of the Society for Ancient Numismatics,* vol. 21, 2002, pp. 41-44; There is much similarity between the Sasanians and the Seleucids since the latter represented themselves to their subjects as descendents of a god (*theos*) and more importantly god-made manifest (*epiphanes*), F.E. Peters, *The Harvest of Hellenism, A History of the Near East from Alexander the Great to the Triumph of Christianity,* Barnes and Noble, New York, 1970 (reprint 1996), p. 232; P.O. Skjærvø has made the observation earlier that these ideas were already current during the time of

part of the Hellenic past of Iran. Alexander and the Seleucids considered themselves as descendants of θεός "god;" and more importantly θεοπάτωρ "of divine descent," which was used by the Arsacids as well,[26] also matching the title of *MNW ctry MN yzd'n* of the early Sasanian inscriptions.[27] As A. Gariboldi has shown, the artistic elements in early Sasanian period may also corroborate this suggestion. For example, in the early rock-reliefs, the image of Ohrmzad and Ardaxšīr I are similar and in the same proportion, suggesting equal status.[28]

Ohrmazd and Ardaxšīr at Naqsh-e Rajab

---

the kings of Persis, 1997, pp.93-104. It must also be noted that while Ardaxšīr and other early Sasanians called themselves *bay* "god" or "lord," written in the ideographic form *'lh*, in such Middle Persian texts as the *Ayādgār ī Zarērān*, Ohrmazd also bears this title as *ohrmazd bay*. This suggests the Sasanian belief in their own divinity.

[26] A. Garibolid, "Royal Ideological Patterns Between Seleucid and Parthian Coins: The Case of θεοπάτωρ," *Commerce and Monetary Systems in the Ancient World: Means of Transmission and Cultural Interaction, Melammu Symposia V*, ed. R. Rollinger and Ch. Ulf with collaboration of K. Schengg, Franz Steiner Veralg, 2004, p. 367.

[27] Daryaee, 2002, p. 42.

[28] A. Gariboldi, "Astral Symbology on Iranian Coinage," *East and West*, vol. 54, 2004, p. 32.

By 224 CE most of the Iranian Plateau[29] and the Arab[30] side of the Persian Gulf had become part of Ardaxšīr's empire.[31] The invasion of Armenia, however, was unsuccessful and the Armenians were able to defeat and halt the Sasanian encroachment.[32] The Armenian sources tell us of this defeat, but the Sasanian sources are silent. To the contrary, a rock relief was carved, suggesting the victory of the Sasanians over the Armenians at Salmās. Ardaxšīr had to devise another way to takeover Armenia, namely court intrigues and the conspiracies to kill the Armenian king.

Ardaxšīr and his army also invaded Syria and Cappadocia, expanding the Sasanian onslaught to the borders of Rome.[33] Thus, he came into open conflict with Rome and Emperor Alexander Severus (222-235 CE), a conflict which proved to have no clear winner.[34] In a letter to Ardaxšīr, Alexander had made it clear that his invasion of the Roman empire would not be as successful as his conquest of his other neighbors.[35] By 233 CE both sides were exhausted, and neither side appear to have won, but Alexander Severus remained in Antioch.[36] While Severus was alive, neither side was able to defeat the other decisively.

---

[29] *Herodian*, Book VI 2, 2.

[30] R.G. Hoyland, *Arabia and the Arabs, From the Bronze Age to the Coming of Islam*, Routledge, London and New York, 2001, pp. 27-28.

[31] Widengren, 1971, pp. 711-782; J. Wiesehöfer, 1987, pp. 371-376.

[32] Armenia was of course independent of Rome, see Dio Cassius, *Dio's Roman History*, Book LXXX, 3, 3.

[33] *Herodian*, Book VI,2,1; Zonares XII.15; Dignas & Winter, p. 71.

[34] Dio Cassius, *Dio's Roman History*, Book LXXX, 3, p. 483.

[35] *Herodian*, Book VI, 2, 4. Eutropius makes Alexander Severus the victor over Ardaxšīr, Eutropius, *Breviarium*, Book VIII.23, translated with an introduction and commentary by H.W. Bird, Liverpool University Press, 1993. The same may be said of the fourth century CE source the *Scriptores Historiae Augustae*, Severus Alexadner 56.2 and 56.5-8; Dignas and Winter, 2007, p. 75.

[36] *Herodian*, Book VI,6,5-6.

When Severus died in 235 CE, Mesopotamia, Dura, Carr-hae, Nisbis and finally Hatra were attacked and successful-ly annexed by the Sasanians.[37] Ardaxšīr then retired and spent the last years of his life in Persis while his son, Šābuhr I who had taken part in the 240 CE campaign con-tinued his conquests and the expansion of the empire. The question might be why Ardaxšīr had taken on these cam-paigns against the Romans? This was probably due to the fact that while the stable borders between the two empires of Rome and Arsacid Iran had been Oshroene, Hatra, and Armenia, when Severus conquered Oshroene, the heart-land of the Arsacid and later Sasanian dynasty was put in danger, prompting the industrious Ardaxšīr to stop and push back the Severan advances.[38]

[37] For a detailed study of the Perso-Roman wars of the third century see, E. Kettenhofen, *Die römisch-persischen Kriege des 3. Jahrhunderts n. Chr. Nach der Inscrift Šāpuhrs I. An der Ka'be-ye Zartošt (ŠKZ)*, Beihefte zum TAVO, Reihe B., Geisteswissenschaften, Nr. 55, Wiesbaden, 1982. In this campaign Šābuhr I, the son of Ardaxšīr, was the main actor, p. 19, Dig-nas and Winter, p. 40.

[38] D.S. Potter, *The Roman Empire at Bay (AD 180-395)*, Routledge, London and New York, 2004, p. 217.

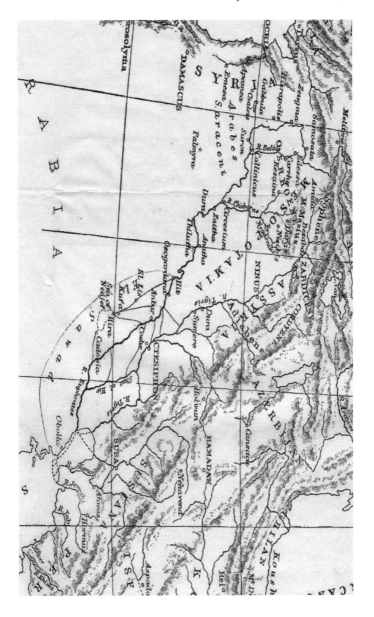

III

Šābuhr I: The Strongest World Empire
in the Third Century

Ardaxšīr's son, Šābuhr I had become his co-regent in 240 CE. This is apparent from a coinage which portrays both men together, probably ordered by Ardaxšīr to ensure a safe succession. This might have been due to the presence of other sons of Ardaxšīr who had been given governorships of other provinces and might have wanted to assume the throne, just as Ardaxšīr himself had done in his youth. This system is characteristic of the Sasanians, under whom sons were sent to rule different provinces and when the king died, one of the heirs assumed the throne. In this manner, there was always a danger of dynastic squabbling, of which the Sasanians had their fair share. The method of succession was initially based on the choice of the preceding king, but later the nobility and the Zoroastrian priests presumed the role of the electors.[1] Šābuhr I had accompanied his father in battles,

---

[1] According to a later source, when the king died, a council chose the next king and the Chief Priest (Persian *mowbed ī mowbedan*) had to agree with the decision, M. Minovi, *Nāma-ye Tansar*, Tehran, 1352, p. 88; and for the English translation see M. Boyce, *The Letter of Tansar*, Rome, 1968, p. 62.

making him battle ready and in fact ensured his success in wars against Rome. Shortly after Šābuhr's succession, Gordian invaded Mesopotamia in 243 CE in order to retrieve what had been taken by Ardaxšīr and his son after Alexander Severus' death. But Šābuhr tells us (in the ŠKZ) that he was able to kill Gordian at Misikhe in 244 CE, close to the Euphrates river, the place he later called *Pērōz-Šābuhr* (Victorious is Šābuhr).[2] It is now known that Gordian had died in Zaitha in northern Mesopotamia in 244 CE at a time when the warfare between the two sides seemed unlikely.[3] Thus, it is suggested by some that after the defeat, the retreating Roman forces murdered Gordian at Zaitha.[4] According to Šābuhr I's Ka'be-ye Zardošt inscription, Gordian had come with a force composed of "Goths and Germans" (ŠKZ Pa4/37 *gwt w grm'ny*), and they were defeated in a frontal battle. Philip the Arab, the new soldier-emperor, was forced to sign a treaty which ceded much territory and a large sum of gold as war reparations, amounting to 500,000 denarii.[5] The territories which the Sasanians were able to take from the Romans were most of Mesopotamia and Armenia.[6] We should not

---

[2] Roman sources are divided as to the cause of death of Gordian. *Oracaula Sibyllina* XIII, 13-20 predicts Gordian's downfall as a betrayal; Aurelius Victor, *liber de Caesaribus* 27, 7-8: 7 states that he was a victim of intrigues of his Praetorian Perfect, Marcus Philippus; Festus, *Breviarium* 22 mentions that Gordian was returning, victorious from his war against the Persians, when he was murdered by Philip. For all these sources see M.H. Dodgeon and S.N.C. Lieu, *The Roman Eastern Frontier and the Persian Wars, A Documentary History*, Routledge, London and New York, 1991, pp. 36-45. For details see Kettenhofen, *op. cit.*, pp. 31-37.

[3] Potter, p. 236.

[4] Potter, p. 236.

[5] ŠKZ 5/4/9.

[6] Zonaras XII, 19; Evagrius, *Historia Ecclesiastica V, 7* which talks only about Armenia, see Dodgeon and Lieu, pp. 45-46.

lose sight of the fact that the newly established Sasanian
dynasty was facing a branch of the Arsacid family in Armenia and so it needed to flush out any such resistance to
secure its northern flank while fighting the Romans. For
this reason, the great kingdom of Armenia was to have a
turbulent history during the Sasanian period.

Šābuhr I commemorated his victory in a rock-relief at
Naqsh-e Rustam showing him subjugating the two Roman
emperors to his will. Šābuhr I has also left us a long biography of his deeds at Ka'be-ye Zardošt, in Persis, which is
the first long testament from the Sasanians themselves and
demonstrates their outlook in an epic narrative. In this *res
gesta*, he provides information on his religious conviction,
lineage, the areas that he ruled over, and also the fate of
the Romans.

Naqsh-e Rustam: Šābuhr I, Valerian and Philip

There, he states that Gordian and his army were destroyed. Šābuhr I also tells us that Caesar lied, putting the
matters in a Zoroastrian doctrinal context where the Romans represented the concept of Lie / Chaos, against the

Persian representatives of Truth / Order.[7] The second campaign began in 252 CE against a Roman force of 60,000 at Barbalissus which ended in total defeat of the Romans, and if we are to believe the ŠKZ narrative, some 37 towns in Mesopotamia and Syria were taken.[8] The motivation for this campaign by Šābuhr I is again explained by the phrase in the ŠKZ: *W kysr TWB MKDBW-t W 'L 'rmn-y wyns 'BD-t* "and Caesar again lied and did wrong to Armenia."[9] What was the lie? In effect, although Philip had promised to allow the Iranian control over Armenia, he did not actually cede Armenia to the Sasanians and only went back to the old treaty agreed upon from the time of Nero where the Roman emperor crowned the Armenian king selected by the Arsacid king of kings.[10] Of course the Arsacid dynasty of Armenia would not have agreed to the continuation of such tradition, nor did the Sasanians liked to see their nemesis to the north being crowned by the Romans.

In 260 CE, Šābuhr I began his third campaign and conquered western Mesopotamia, Syria,[11] and the coast of eastern Mediterranean. At this war, Emperor Valerian along with some senators and soldiers were captured and

---

[7] The concept of lie (druɣ) is antithetical to the ancient Iranian ethics and the idea of order and righteousness (*aša*), see M. Boyce, *Zoroastrianism, Its Antiquity and Constant Vigour*, Columbia Lectures on Iranian Studies, Mazda Publishers, Costa Mesa, California, 1992, pp. 56-57. For a study of the Achaemenid precedence of this concept in royal idealogy and its relation to religion, see Bruce Lincoln, *Religion, Empire, and Torture*, University of Chicago Press, 2007.

[8] ŠKZ 12/9/11.

[9] ŠKZ 6/4/10. For the campaign see Kettenhofen, pp. 38-46.

[10] Potter., p. 237.

[11] In regards to the idea that the Sasanians may have claimed Syria, that is the cities of Carrhae, Edessa and Nisibis, by ancestral (Arsacid) rights see Z. Rubin, "The Roman Empire in the Res Gestae Divi Saporis," *Ancient Iran and the Mediterranean World*, ed. E. Dąbrowa, *Electrum* 2, Jagiellonian University Press, Kraków, 1998, pp. 183-185.

deported to the Sasanian territory.[12] Now Goths, Romans,
Slavs and other people from the Near East were incorpo-
rated into the Sasanian empire. No other person before
could have claimed that he was able to kill a Roman emperor, make one a tributary, and capture and imprison the
third. Šābuhr was very much aware of his feat and did not
hesitate to mention it in his inscription. At a rock-relief in
Persis, Valerian is shown kneeling before him, and today
among the ruins of the city of Bēšābuhr, a place is marked
as *zendan-e valerian* "Valerian's prison." This victory by
Šābuhr I did not escape the attention of Roman sources
either, although the reason for Valerian's defeat, as many
Christian writers recorded it, was his paganism and tor-
menting of Christians, although others gave a more sober
view of the captured emperor. [13]

Bēšābuhr relief

[12] For the details (including maps) of the campaign and the cities taken
by Šābuhr I see Kettenhofen, *op. cit.*, pp. 97-126; ŠKZ 15/11/24-25.
[13] For example Lactantius, *de mortibus persecutorum* 5; Eusebius, *Historia
ecclesiastics*, VII, 13, and especially Orosius, *adversus paganos*, see Dodgeson and Lieu, pp. 58-65.

Although the borders between Rome and Iran fluctuated between the Tigris and the Euphrates, depending on the military success on either side, this did not mean that travel was restricted. In fact, people from both sides traveled from one side to another, engaged in trade, and intermarried. This openness and ease of movement from one side of the border to another made spies useful, and supplying information on the enemy was seen as a great betrayal by both sides.[14] For now, Mesopotamia was in the Iranian hands, but Armenia needed to be dealt with as it had resisted Ardaxšīr and defeated his army.

Armenia was to be the main bone of contempt between the Iranians and the Romans and remained so until the end of the Sasanian period. The Armenian situation was much more complex and important for both sides, because of the strategic and economic interests, and Armenia served as a buffer between Iran and Rome. At the same time, when a branch of the Arsacid royal family remained in Armenia, enough reason was handed to Šābuhr to put an end to the situation. He planned the assassination of king Xosrov and installed another king loyal to him, named Tirdates (Tirdād, Arm. Trdt) who ruled from 252-262 CE. Armenia's importance for the Iranians is quite obvious, as several of the heirs to the Sasanian throne would be the princes who were stationed in Armenia and were called *wuzurg-arman-šāh* "The Great King of Armenia."[15] No other province of the Sasanian empire had such an important title attached to it.

---

[14] For the issue of borders and frontiers between Rome and Persia see H. Elton, *Frontiers of the Roman Empire*, Indiana University Press, Bloomington and Indianapolis, 1996, pp. 97-99.

[15] Agathangełos, *History of the Armenians*, Translation and Commentary by R.W. Thomson, State University of New York Press, Albany, 1976, p. 35.

During Šābuhr's reign, his religious outlook was also a matter of importance. The Zoroastrian "church" was being formed by Kerdīr who was trying to establish a body of law, canonize the *Avesta*, create a common doctrine, unify the belief system, and establish a Zoroastrian religious hierarchy tied to the State. At the same time, Mānī emerged from Mesopotamia, professing a religion which by all accounts was universal. Manichaean sources state that during the last years of Ardaxšīr's reign, Mānī had crossed the empire and had gone to India. During the reign of Šābuhr I he came back to the Sasanian empire, appeared before the king and was honored, staying with the king for sometime and was given permission to preach throughout the empire.[16]

At this time it would be wrong to see Zoroastrianism as an exclusive religion, since it was still a religion that could be adopted by the conquered people. Šābuhr's tolerance of Mānī, and at the same time his commitment to Ohrmazd and Zoroastrianism has caused problems for historians. But if Šābuhr saw the growing power and structure of the Zoroastrian priesthood, might he not have attempted to show them that the King of Kings was still the one who has the last say? Were it not the Sasanians who were the caretakers and priests of the Anāhīd temple and were schooled in the rites and ceremonies? One can argue that the Sasanian concern with politics did not necessarily diminish their religious authority, at least until the time of Wahrām I. Mānī was then able to propagate his religion during Šābuhr I's rule and that of his son. Still, Šābuhr mentions in his *res gestae* that many Wahrām fires were established and that lamb, wine, and bread were offered to the gods for the soul of the kings and queens of the family

---

[16] *The Kephalaia of the Teacher*, ed. I. Gardner, E.J. Brill, Leiden, 1995, 15.28, p. 21.

of Sāsān. All of these, including the King's cult, might have seemed "pagan" to a Zoroastrian priest.

If one compares the retinue, the bureaucracy and the size of the courts of Ardaxšīr I and Šābuhr I, one can observe an increase in the administrative apparatus and the bureaucracy, including the size of the court. This would be natural, since if an empire was to be centralized and to be functioning, it needed to have not only a king, but also governors (*šahrābān*), viceroys (*bidaxšān*), a steward of royal property (*framādār*) a commander of the royal guard (*hazārbed*), scribes (*dibīrān*), treasurers (*ganzwarān*), judges (*dādwarān*), and a market inspector (*wāzārbed*), along with the local kings (*šahrdārān*), princes of royal blood (*wāspuhragān*), grandees (*wuzurgān*), minor nobility (*āzādān*), and other officials as mentioned in the ŠKZ. The nobility (*wuzurgān*), whose loyalty to their clan was paramount, now submitted to the Sasanians.[17] Such families as Warāz, Sūren, Andēgān, Kāren, and others were given various honors and positions, such as being master of ceremonies or crown bestowers. They also displayed their clan emblem or coat-of-arms on their caps (*kulāfs*) as is apparent on the rock-reliefs at Naqsh-e Rajab and Naqsh-e Rustam. We do not know which symbol belonged to which clan and what the symbols exactly meant, whether insignias or names of the clans made into designs.

---

[17] For a list of the functionaries at the Sasanian court in the third century see R.N. Frye, "Notes on the early Sassanian State and Church," *Studi Orientalistici in onore di Giorgio Levi Della Vida*, Rome, 1956, pp. 314-335.

Šābuhr I

IV

Jousting for Kingship: Wahrāms and Narsē

The next king, Hormizd I (271-272 CE), the youngest son of Šābuhr I came to the throne and ruled a short time.[1] He was associated with good rule and the building of the city of Rām-Hormizd in Xūzestān. The Ka'be-ye Zardošt inscription (ŠKZ) calls him the Great king of Armenia (*wuzurg-arman-šāh*) during the rule of his father. To be king of Armenia in the third century seems to have been a position of privilege and usually signaled the fact that the person occupying the seat was the heir apparent to the Sasanian throne. Tabarī states that Hormizd I was fearless and showed extreme loyalty to his father. He had shown military talent during Šābuhr's campaign in the 250's which gave reasons for the king to appoint him as heir.[2] He was involved in the wars with the Romans in Syria, Cilicia and Cappadocia during his father's second campaign.[3] He then joined Šābhur I in the conquest of An-

[1] Agathias IV, 24, 5.
[2] M.-L. Chaumont, "Les grands rois sassanides d'Arménie (IIIéme siécle ap. J.-C.)," *Iranica Antiqua*, vol. 8, 1968, p. 82.
[3] Kettenhofen, 1982, p. 68.

tioch in the early 250s.[4] He was chosen over his elder brother Narsē, who in the ŠKZ was called king of Sīstān (*Sagān-šāh*), and Šābuhr king of Mesene (*Mēšān-šāh*).

Religiously, it is not clear why Hormizd I had allowed Mānī to preach his message freely and also let Kerdīr continue his activity, giving him new ranks through the ceremonial cap and belt (*kulāf ud kamar*). In the Manichaean sources it is said that Hormizd I met Mānī,[5] was impressed by him and his message,[6] and allowed him to travel freely to Mesopotamia. This may have been part of his campaign of dual containment, controlling both religions that were attempting to dominate the region. Wahrām I (271-274 CE), Hormizd's successor and brother, had a relatively short rule as well, although we have more information about him and his eventful career. He was the eldest son of Šābuhr I, but had been passed over in favor of Hormizd. He had been appointed the king of Gēlān by his father. Initially, Kerdīr appears to have backed his succession and consequently the Zoroastrian priesthood and the person of Kerdīr benefited from his succession in 274 CE. It was at this time that Mānī was sent from the east to present himself to Wahrām, and we have a Manichaean text which describes the harsh treatment of the prophet. He was scolded for not being a good doctor or having any benefit, and Wahrām ordered his arrest and imprisonment.

---

[4] M.R. Shayegan, "Hormozd I," *Encycelopaedia Iranica*, Vol XII, pp. 462-464

[5] N. Sims-Williams, "The Sogdian Fragment of Leningrad II: Mani at the Court of the Shahanshah," *Bulletin of the Asia Institute*, vol. 4, 1990, p. 283.

[6] W. Sundermann, *Mitteliranische manichäische Texte kirchengeschichtlichen Inhalts*, Berlin, 1981, p. 129; Sims-Williams, *ibid.*, pp. 281-288.

Kerdīr

Wahrām II, who came to the throne in 274 CE, may have needed Kerdīr's support in bypassing his uncle Narsē, who was now the Great King of Armenia. It is in this period that Kerdīr began his real ascent to power. Kerdīr also started the persecution of non-Zoroastrians in the empire, among them Jews, Christians, Manichaeans, Mandeans and Buddhists. During the rule of Wahrām II (274-293 CE) Kerdīr achieved higher ranks and status, and it is during this period that the Sasanian kings lost much of their religious power as caretakers of the Anāhīd temple to Kerdīr, making him the judge and high priest of the whole empire. This meant that from then on, the priests acted as judges throughout the empire and probably court cases were based on Zoroastrian law, except when members of other religious minorities had disputes with each other.[7] Wahrām II is also the first ruler to have a family portrait struck on his coins. On his *drahms* (silver coins) he is shown with his queen Šābuhrduxtag who was his cousin and his son, Wahrām III.[8] He also had several rock-reliefs of himself and his family carved as memorials. This is an interesting feature of Wahrām II in that he was very much

---

[7] For the role of the priests in the Sasanian period see Sh. Shaked, "Administrative Functions of Priests in the Sasanian Period," *Proceedings of the First European Conference of Iranian Studies*, 1990, pp. 261-273.

[8] J.K. Choksy, "A Sasanian Monarch, His Queen, Crown Prince and Deities: The Coinage of Wahram II," *American Journal of Numismatics*, vol. I, 1989, pp. 117-137.

determined to leave a portrait of his family[9], an insistence which incidentally gives us much information about the court and the Persian concept of royal banquet (*bazm*).[10]

The *Bazm* included wine drinking, feasting, music and games being played before the king and the courtiers as evidenced not only from the rock reliefs, but also the silver dishes from the Sasanian period. While the term *bazm* means "feast," the Armenian sources give us its true usage during the Sasanian period. Armenian *bazmoc'k'* "to recline," meant a banqueting-couch which the nobility and the king used during the court feasting. The courtiers would recline on cushions (*barj*), where the number of the cushions signified their importance in the court. Some of these banqueting couches had room for two people, referred to as *taxt* or *gāh* where one's proximity to the king of kings showed his/her honor and closeness to him.[11] Naturally, the further one's *taxt* or *gāh* was from the king, the lesser his rank, and if moved even further away, it was a sign of demotion and disgrace. These portraits may also have been a means of justifying Wahrām II's succession over Narsē who by now must have been quite dissatisfied from being bypassed several times, although he was the Great King of Armenia, a title reserved for the heir to the throne. Wahram II's precarious situation is also clear from the revolt of his brother, Hormizd, in Sīstān in 283 CE. Although the chronology of the events is not clear, we know

---

[9] A.Sh. Shahbazi, "Studies in Sasanian Prosopography: III Barm-i Dilak: Symbolism of Offering Flowers," *The Art and Archaeology of Ancient Persia*, ed. V. Sarkhosh, et. al., I.B. Tauris, London, 1998, pp. 58-66.

[10] The only detailed study of the concept of *bazm* and the idea of its significance is that by A.S. Melikian-Chirvani, "The Iranian bazm in Early Persian Sources," *Banquets d'Orient*, ed. R. Gyselen, Res Orientales IV, Bures-sur-Yvette, 1992, pp. 95-120.

[11] N. Garsoian, *The Epic Histories: Buzandaran Patmut'iwnk'*, p. 515; for feasting under Šāpuhr II see Chapter IV.XVI, p. 146.

that Hormizd was supported by the Sīstānīs, Gēlānīs and the Kušāns (Rufii)[12] in his campaign against Wahrām II.[13] This was not the only problem that Wahrām II had to face, as we hear of religious strife as well, namely in the province of Xūzestān, where a revolt was led by a certain mowbed who held power there for some time.[14]

Wahrām II and the court

On the Roman front, there were plans already made by Probus to invade the Sasanian territories, but after his death, the war was continued by Carus who invaded Mesopotamia, laying siege to the capital Ctesiphon while Wahrām II was in the East. However, Carus died in Mesopotamia in 283 CE.[15] Diocletian, who had to deal with the internal problems of Rome, made a treaty with Wahrām II, ensuring the Perso-Roman borders. Now Wahrām II could

---

[12] Likely a mistake for *Cusii,* the Kushans, see Dodgeson and Lieu, *op. cit.,* p. 373.

[13] *Panegyrici Latini,* III/11, 17, 2, Dodgeon and Lieu, *op. cit.,* p. 112.

[14] *Die Chronik von Arbela,* 8,66, ed. P. Kawerau, Peeters, Louvan, 1985.

[15] Most sources claim that while Carus was successful, he was struck by lightning. For example see Eutropis, *Breviarium,* IX, 18, 1.

deal with his brother Hormizd and Diocletian was able to focus his attention on the reforms in his empire, bringing order to an otherwise chaotic Roman realm. The new treaty divided Armenia among the two powers and left western Armenia in the hands of Tirdat (Tirdates IV) while Narsē ruled over greater Armenia, now commonly known as *Persarmenia*. By 293 CE, when Wahrām II died, his rival Hormizd had been pacified in the east, but dynastic squabbling continued regardless. Wahrām III, son of Wahrām II, was known as King of the Sakas (*sagān-šāh*)[16] and he was brought to the throne by a court faction, perhaps with the backing of Kerdīr, Adur-Farrobāy, king of Mēšān, and Wahnām, son of Tartus. However, Narsē was not going to be passed over yet again. He left for Mesopotamia and was met by a group of nobles who had given their allegiance to him. We do not know what happened to Wahrām III, but Wahnām was captured and executed and Narsē finally became king of kings.

Again Narsē has blessed us by leaving his personal account of the events on a monument at Paikuli in northern Mesopotamia. It is a biography and a narrative justifying his succession to the throne in which it is claimed that the nobility and courtiers asked him to take the throne when he met them.[17] The similarities between this inscription and the others in the Near East, such as the Behistun inscription of Darius I and even some pre-Achaemenid ones, has given some the reason to believe that it is less reliable source. In fact, recently it has been claimed that the Paikuli inscription may be devoid of much historical information because it belongs to the genre of epic literature which enjoys a long history in ancient Near East. However, one can

---

[16] Agathias also provides the same title for Wahrām III, IV, 24, 6-8.

[17] P.O. Skjærvø and H. Humbach, *The Sassanian Inscription of Paikuli*, Wiesbaden, 1983, p. 44 (Parthian: line 18).

scarcely accept this assumption, and while it is ceded that the story is told in an epic setting (formula, *topos*), there are only so many ways in which a king could have related his story and his campaign. Relating a story or historical event in a specific form or formula should not necessarily deplete the story of its historical significance.[18] After all, kings waged wars, defeated their enemies, and ruled over their kingdoms. These issues in themselves are the genre that gives cause to a king to commission an inscription.

Narsē and Anāhīd

It is worth noticing that a constant feature of the Iranian civilization recurs here, one with precedence in the Behis-

---

[18] S. Mori contends that the Paikuli inscription is basically relating the traditional Near Eastern story of how a king achieves supremacy with the aid of the gods in the epic form. He also believes that the early Islamic texts, such as al-Tabarī are of little use for the history of the Sasanian period, "The narrative structure of the Paikuli Inscription," *Orient*, vol. 30-31, 1995, pp. 182-193. I wonder if then we should rely solely on the Greco-Roman sources if our historical inscriptions and the Sasanian royal chronicle are of little use for understanding Sasanian history!

tun and the Naqsh-e Rustam inscriptions. In the Paikuli inscription we come across the notion that the enemies of the rightful king (Narsē, follower of Truth/Order) were followers of Lie (demon/Chaos).[19] This binary opposition, a hallmark of Sasanian Zoroastrianism, worked well in demonizing the king's enemies. Narsē's rock-relief at Naqsh-e Rustam is also important as it shows him receiving the symbol of sovereignty from the goddess, Anāhīd.[20] Leaving the religious implications aside, could this mean that politically Narsē was able to regain the control of the temple of Anāhīd at Istakhr and was re-orienting his devotion to this deity at the cost of Kerdīr's power? Of course, it is possible that devotion to Lady Anāhīd was never forsaken, but I think the mere representation of Narsē along with Anāhīd may hint at a significant religio-political change in the Sasanian empire. This perhaps reaffirmed the tradition of Narsē's father and grandfather, Šābuhr I and Ardaxšīr I, and now Narsē himself, as the legitimate rulers who began their campaigns supported by the cult of this goddess.

On the international front, Narsē was far less successful. He declared war on Rome in 296 CE because of the Roman meddling in Armenia. Diocletian sent an army under Galerius, and while initially the Iranians held the upper hand, in the second battle in Armenia at Satala the Sasanian army was routed and Narsē lost his wife and family and barely escaped being captured.[21] In 298, Narsē negotiated a peace treaty (Treaty of Nisibis) where in exchange for his

---

[19] Skjærvø, *Paikuli*, p. 44: line 18.

[20] A.Sh. Shahbazi, "Narse's Relief at Naqš-i Rustam," *Archäologische Mitteilungen aus Iran*, vol. 16, 1983, pp. 255-268.

[21] Lactantius, *de mortibus persecutorum*, 9, 6-8 provides an insight into Galerius' invasion via Armenia and his capture of Narsē's belongings, Dodgeon and Lieu., p. 125.

family's return and peace, he ceded parts of Mesopotamia, restored Armenia to Tirdat, and agreed to the selection of the King of Iberia by the Romans.[22] This Roman influence in Iberia (Georgia) was to be detrimental to Sasanian influence in the region, since in 330 CE the Georgian king and nobility adopted Christianity. Narsē's rule thus brought about a new balance of power between the Romans and the Iranians. This weakness in imperial aspiration may be apparent from the omission of *an-Ērān* from Narsē's titles on some of the coin legends.

To reassess, in the third century CE, the first two Sasanian rulers of *Ērānšahr* established and organized an empire from the province of Persis. In the third century, Persis appears to have had a centrality, not only because it is the first province that all of the early Sasanian rock reliefs mention, but also because of its position as the home of the family of Sāsān. From the later sources we also learn that just like Constantine in the fourth century, Ardaxšīr I also attempted to establish a state religion, a religion that he and his ancestors followed and is called *mazdēsn* or Mazda-worshipping-religion (*i.e.*, Zoroastrianism). This is the first word that appears on the coins and inscription of Ardaxšīr and Šābuhr, suggesting their deep devotion to Ohrmazd. Ardaxšīr, along with his wise priest, Tōsar (alt. Tansar) sifted through the existing oral and written tradition of the empire, particularly those in Persis, and began the canonization of the doctrines of what is today called Zoroastrianism. By the time of Šābuhr I, the Romans had realized that a new power existed in the East which could defeat any Roman army and even kill its generals and hold captive its emperors. Šābuhr I's inscription also demonstrates the fact that the administrative apparatus of the Sasanian empire

---

[22] Petrus Patricuius, *frag. 14, FGH IV*, p. 189, Dodgeson and Lieu, p. 133.

had grown and become more sophisticated. This is to be expected if an organized and vibrant empire was to exist. Šābuhr I, however, also tried to use Manichaeism - a religion which seems to have attracted many from different regions in Asia and the Mediterranean world - as an alternative to Zoroastrianism. While Zoroastrianism was the religion of his father and forefathers, Šābuhr I understood that in order to have a universal empire, a universal religion capable of cementing loyalty to the king and state was desirable. To be the ruler of the Iranians was one matter, but to rule over *an-Ērān*, one needed a more universal religion.

The growing number of Zoroastrian priests, however, would not allow this to happen. After Šābuhr's death, under Wahrām I, Kerdīr and company made sure that Mānī is stopped, imprisoned, and later meets an early death. In this way, the king of kings remained a *mazdēsn* and the Zoroastrian religion spread all over the empire. In a way, Kerdīr is responsible for the preservation of the Zoroastrian tradition that was to come to its full development under later Sasanians. Šābuhr I may have begun to imagine that the concept of *Ērānšahr* need not necessarily be tied to Zoroastrianism (although it had its origin in that tradition) and that any citizen, i.e., *mard ī šahr* "male citizen" / *zan ī šahr* "female citizen," would be considered an *Ērānagān* "Iranian." This idea was to take hold in another century or so, but it was too early for it to be realized in the new empire. Meanwhile, the Zoroastrian priests not only made themselves an important part of the imperial government, but also become evermore involved in the daily affairs of the society. They also reduced the religious power of the king of kings, especially after Šābuhr I's "ungodly" meddling with Mānī. If Zoroastrianism was to survive, it needed to have a hierarchy and a religious tradition codified in the *Avesta* and zealously maintained. While the Wahrāms caved into these demands, Narsē struck back and attempted to make the family of Sāsān the ultimate decision makers. Thus, by the end of the third century CE, equilibrium was reached between the church and the state, neither one being able to really exist without the other or to overtake the other.

Internationally, Rome now had to face a new and more centralized empire which had specific geo-political agendas and did not fear the conflict with the Mediterranean empire. The nature of Rome's presence in Syria and more importantly in Mesopotamia was essentially imperialistic. Since Mesopotamia served as the heartland of the Sasanian empire and housed its capital at Ctesiphon, and was an agricultural center along with Xūzestān, the presence of Roman forts only a short distance to the west made Sasanians weary. This may be the prime reason for the early campaigns of Ardaxšīr and Šābuhr I against the Roman holdings in these regions. In the east, we are not so clear on the Sasanian campaigns, but it is certain that they were able to establish a strong foothold there and secure their border against the Kušāns.

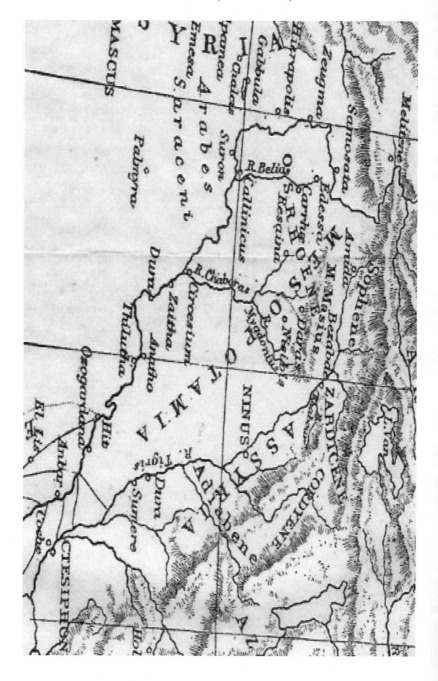

V

Šābuhr II and the Sasanian Rulers
in the Fourth Century

Hormizd II (303-309 CE) succeeded his father Narsē, but did not achieve much militarily, although he did send troops into Syria, deposing the Ghassanid king who was seen as a Roman ally.[1] During Hormizd's reign, Armenia, under the rule of King Tirdates IV, adopted Christianity. Hormizd had tried to improve the Iranian-Armenian relations by marrying his daughter Hormizdduxtag to the Armenian prince Wahan Mamikonian,[2] and such an alliance must have affected the loyalties of some of the Armenian noble families. However, following Tirdat's conversion, some of the Armenian feudal clans (*naxarars*) also converted and supported Tirdat against those *naxarars* loyal to the Sasanians who continued to honor the ancient Mazdean / Zoroastrian tradition of Armenia. It has usually been the case that Armenians have seen this momentous event as a break from the

---

[1] A.Sh. Shahbazi, "Hormozd II," *Encyclopaedia Iranica*, Vol. XII, pp. 464-5.

[2] Buzandaran Patmut'iwnk', *The Epic Histories Attributed to P'awstos Buzand*, Epic Histories IV.50-59.

old "pagan" past, when the Armenian nation and identity was established through the medium of Christianity. But one can also look at this occasion in another way, namely through the eyes of those Armenians who did not convert to the new religion. Those Armenians who chose to stay faithful to their ancient heritage went down the Armenian historiography as either villains or worshipers of *Ormizd, Anāhit,* and *Vahagn.* Christian historians then attempted to erase them from the Armenian historical memory, except for those who were allowed to survive as evil-doers.[3]

For many Armenian *naxarars,* their past history and religion must have meant something important and the adoption of new ways and religion (Christianity) must have not been accepted easily. After all, according to these Armenian nobles, it was King Tirdat who was the heretic adopting a religion from the West, supplanting the Armenian Mazdeans who had been worshipping Ohrmazd since the sixth century BCE. In the scholarly realm, J.R. Russell has put an end to the modern Armenian notion of a pagan past vs. Christianity. According to Armenian historiography, which is Christian and hostile to Zoroastrianism, Armenia was pagan, illiterate and disunited, but when in the early fourth century Christianity was adopted, there emerged a united people or "nation" that held a united vision. Russell has shown that the Armenians from ancient times were a people who, although with a culture under Iranian and Zoroastrian influence, had its own view of what Zoroastrianism meant and gave it an Armenian out-

---

[3] Armazd, Anahīt, Vahagn (Ohrmazd, Anāhīd, and Wahrām, respectively) were initially proclaimed by Tirdat in opposition to the Persians. This demonstrates that the Armenians did not see these deities as specifically Iranian, Agathangełos, pp. 51-53. These deities are also equated with Zeus, Artemis, and Heracles.

look.[4] So the few "evil" *naxarars* mentioned in the Armenian historical narratives, those supporting the Sasanians, were in fact choosing to keep their ancient Armenian tradition at the expense of the new belief. The issue of the future of Armenia was not to be decided at this time and the adoption of Christianity further caused problems and divided the Armenian society for some time to come.

When Hormizd II died, his son Adur-Narsē ruled briefly before being deposed by the nobility and the priests. Instead, the infant son of Hormizd II, Šābuhr II (309-379 CE) was put on the throne.[5] In regards to this king, we have the legend that the courtiers and the clergy placed the crown on his mother's belly when she was pregnant. We may assume that during the early years of his reign, the court and the Zoroastrian priests ran the empire and the empire was secure and stable structurally and administratively to survive without a strong monarch. This might have also signaled the courtiers and the nobility that the empire could be managed without a powerful king, something that would benefit them. However, the Arabs in eastern Arabia were raiding the southwestern provinces of the Sasanian empire, while Constantine and the other emperors battled for the soul of the Roman empire which made the Iranians safe from the western front. When Šābuhr II had come of age (325 CE), he took revenge on the Arabs and hence received the title "the one who pierces shoulders" (Arabic *Dhū al-Aktāf*), referring to the punishment inflicted on the Arab tribes. As a result of his campaigns, some of the Arabs were pushed into the heartland of Arabia and the Persian Gulf region remained in the hands of the Sasanian empire, realizing their overall strat-

---

[4] J.R. Russell, *Zoroastrianism in Armenia*, Harvard Iranian Series, Cambridge, Massachusetts, 1987.

[5] T. Daryaee, "Šapur II," *Encyclopaedia Iranica* (forthcoming 2008).

egy of securing the Persian Gulf. Some Arab tribes were forcibly displaced and relocated into the Sasanian empire. The Taghlīb tribe was settled in Darayn (a port in Bahrayn) and al-Khatt; the Abd al-Qays and Tamīm were settled in Hajar, and the tribe of Bakr b. Wa'īl was settled in Kermān and the Hanazīla in Ramila (vicinity of Ahwaz).[6] To keep the Arabs from mounting further attacks, Šābuhr II constructed a defensive system which was called *war ī tāzīgān* "wall of the Arabs."[7] This wall appears to have been close to the city of Hīra, coming to be known as *Khandaq ī Shapur* (Ditch of Šābuhr).[8]

Thus the relation between the Arabs and Iranians was just not on the frontiers, but also within the Sasanian empire.[9] This is also the first time we hear of the Chionite (*Xyōn*) tribes encroaching on the empire from Central Asia. Šābuhr II was however able to contain and make peace with them.[10] He then placed his son, who now took the title of "King of Kušān" (*kušān-šāh*), on the throne of the east as is evidenced by the coins and a few inscriptions in the Kušān territory.

On the western front, with the conversion of the Armenia to Christianity and the Roman backing of Armenia, Šābuhr II was forced to undertake a new campaign against them. Thus, with the ascent of Constantius to the Roman

---

[6] Meskaweyh, 1369, p. 135; Tabarī, 1999, p. 56

[7] *Šahrestānīhā ī Ērānšahr*, ed. T. Daryaee, Costa Mesa, 2002, passage 43.

[8] R.N. Frye, "The Sasanian System of Walls for Defense," *Studies in Memory of Gaston Wiet*, ed. M. Rosen-Ayalon, Jerusalem, 1977 (reprinted) *Islamic Iran and Central Asia (7th-12th Centuries)*, Variorum Reprints, London, 1979, pp. 8-11; and H. Mahamedi, "Wall as a System of Frontier Defense during the Sasanid Period," *Mēnōg ī Xrad: The Spirit of Wisdom, Essays in Memory of Ahmad Tafazzolī*, ed. T. Daryaee and M. Omidsalar, Mazda Publishers, Costa Mesa, 2004, pp. 156-158.

[9] Hoyland, 2001, p. 28.

[10] Ammianus Marcellinus, Book XVII.5.1.

throne (337 CE), war began and in 338 CE Šābuhr II managed to lay siege to Nisïbis several times. Amida and Singara were in turn captured in 359.[11] The Roman defensive system of fortresses and *limes* hindered Šābuhr's campaign in the region, but some forts such as Vitra fell to him.[12] However, the encroachment of the nomadic tribes of Central Asia forced Šābuhr II to turn his attention to the East,[13] and the war with Rome ended in a stalemate by 356 CE. Around this time, we first hear of the Hunnic tribes, who were probably the Kidarites (Chinese *Jiduolo*), making inroads into the Sasanian empire and also menacing the Gupta empire (320-500 CE) of India. Šābuhr II, who had just returned from the Syrian front, was able to contain his eastern foes by making an alliance with their king, Grumbates, against the Romans. By such action, he secured an ally for future attacks against the Romans.[14]

It is quite possible that it was Šābuhr II who defeated his eastern foes and established the Sasanian dominion over the Kušāns.[15] This theory can be substantiated from the two Middle Persian inscriptions which mention that the eastern boundary of the Sasanian empire under Šābuhr II included Sind, Sīstān, and Turān.[16]

---

[11] Festus 27.1-2; Dignas & Winter, pp. 89-90.

[12] Ammianus Marcellinus XX.7.9.

[13] *Die Chronik von Arbela* 1985, 85.

[14] Ammianus Marcellinus XVII.5.1.

[15] M. Azarnoush, *The Sasanian Manor House at Hājīābād, Iran*, Casa Editrice Le Lettere, Fierenze, 1994, p. 14.

[16] Šābuhr II's Persepolis inscription, Ps-I.3, M. Back, *Die Sassanidischen Staatsinschriften*, E.J. Brill, Leiden, 1978, pp. 490-492.

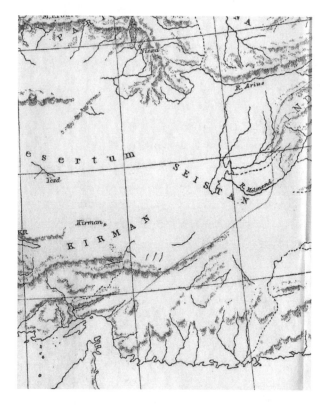

Ammianus Marcellinus also lists the provinces of the Sasanian empire in that period as Assyria, Susiana, Media, Persis, Parthia, Greater Carmania, Hyrcania, Margiana, the Bactriani, the Sogdiani, the Sacae, and Scythia at the foot of Imaus (Himalayas), and beyond the same mountain, Serica, Aria, the Paropanisadae, Drangiana, Arachosia, and Gedrosia.[17] Tabarī, additionally, mentions that among his city building projects, Šābuhr II established cities in Sind and Sīstān,[18] which confirms his rule over that region. Finally, most of the gold coins minted by Šābuhr II are from eastern mints such as Marw where the Kušāns also minted gold coins. Also, a large amount of copper coins from the

---

[17] Ammianus Marcellinus, XXIII.6.14.
[18] Tabarī, 1999, p. 65.

mints of Sakastān/Sīstān and Kabul exist.[19] This may mean that Šābuhr II was able to extract a large amount of gold and other precious metals from his defeated eastern enemies.

Šābuhr II at Bēšābuhr

In 359 CE Šābuhr II, with the backing of king Grumbates, attacked Syria, laid siege to Amida, and entered it after seventy three days[20]. The city was sacked and its population deported to Xūzestān as punishment because the son of the Kidirite king was killed in the siege. In 361 CE, the new Roman emperor, Julian, counter-attacked and won against Šābuhr II with victories in 363 CE, and even laid siege to Ctesiphon. The capital, however, was not taken because of disorder and pillaging among the Roman forces.[21] In anticipation of Julian's victory against the Persians an inscription was placed in upper Jordan valley, with the premature title of BARORVM EXTINCTORI, probably because at his initial success in Antioch in March

[19] N. Schindel, *Sylloge Nummorum Sasanidarum, Shapur II.-Kawad* I, 3/1 & 3/2, Verlag der Österreichischen Akademie der Wissenschaften, Wien, 2004, p. 26.
[20] Ammianus Marcellinus XVIII.9.
[21] Libanius, *Selected Orations*, vol. I, translated by A.F. Norman, Cambridge University Press, London 1969 (reprint 2003). xviii.254-255.

of 363.[22] We are told that among the Roman generals there was a Persian renegade by the name of Hormizd who commanded the cavalry. Julian had destroyed his own naval ships, so that his forces could not retreat,[23] and Šābuhr II responded by adopting a scorched-earth strategy in Mesopotamia which resulted in widespread hunger among the Roman forces. In June of 363, Iranian forces equipped with elephants defeated the Romans, and Julian was badly wounded in the battle, probably by a "cavalry spearmen," and died in his tent.[24] Eutropius, who was an eyewitness to this campaign, affirms that Julian was killed at the hand of the enemy.[25]

Subsequently, Jovian was elected emperor and had to make a peace treaty with Šābuhr II, which the Romans called *ignobili decreto* "shameful treaty,"[26] ceding eastern Mesopotamia, Armenia and the adjoining regions, fifteen fortresses in total, as well as Nisibis.[27] Iranian terms and conditions were conveyed by Surena (Sūren) who agreed to have the mainly Christian population of Nisibis moved to the Roman territory while the Iranian standard was raised over the city.[28] Jovian left Mesopotamia and the Romans were not to engage the Sasanians further, as the succeeding Emperor Valens had to deal with the Germanic tribes in the Balkans.

---

[22] G.W. Bowersock, *Julian the Apostate*, Harvard University Press, Cambridge, Massachusetts, 1978, pp. 123-124.

[23] Libanius xviii.263.

[24] Ammianus Marcellinus XXV.3.6 ; Libanius xviii.269-270.

[25] Eutropius, *Breviarium* X.16.

[26] Ammianus Marcellinus XXV.7.13.

[27] Ammianus Marcellinus XXV.7.9.

[28] For Šābuhr II's wars see Dignas and Winter, pp. 51-54; Chronicon Paschale 554.

King Tiran, who had attempted to keep Armenia independent by playing both the Romans and the Iranians, lost his life to Šābuhr II. He was replaced by his son, Aršak II (350-367 CE) who initially also tried to appease both the Romans and the Iranians, but finally joined Julian's failed expedition against the Sasanians.[29] As part of the peace treaty between Šābuhr II and Jovian, Armenia and Georgia were to come under Sasanian control and the Romans were not to get involved in Armenian affairs.[30] The Armenian king was captured by the Sasanians and imprisoned in the Castle of Oblivion (Fortress of Andeməš or Castle of Anyuš in Xūzestān), where he is said to have committed suicide while being visited by his eunuch Drastamat.[31] The cities of Artašat, Vałaršapat, Eruandašat, Zarehawan, Zarišat, Van and Naxčwan were taken and their populations deported, among whom many were Jewish families.[32] The pro-Iranian *naxarars*, namely Vahan Mamikonean and Meružan Arcruni accompanied Šābūhr II and were rewarded for their help, and two Iranians, Zik and Karēn along with a large army were placed over Armenian affairs.[33] Georgia was also placed under the Iranian control where Šābuhr II installed Aspacures in eastern Georgia, but eventually the Roman emperor Valens succeeded in installing Sauromaces in western Georgia.[34]

---

[29] Ammianus Marcellinus xxiii.3.5 : xxiv.7.8.

[30] Ammianus Marcellinus xxv.7.12.

[31] Buzandaran Patmut'iwnk', Epic Histories V.vii.

[32] Epic Histories IV.lv.

[33] Epic Histories IV.lviii.

[34] Ammianus Marcellinus xxvii.12.15.

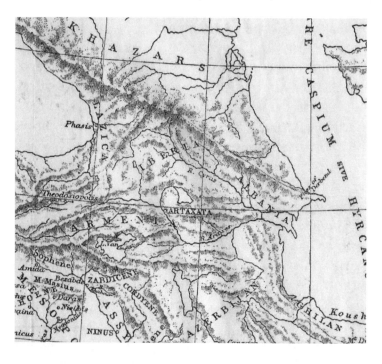

Pap (367-374 CE), the son of the Armenian ruler Aršak who had fled to the Romans, was placed on the throne in 367 CE with the Roman backing. He was able to withstand Šābuhr II's attack near Bagawan in 371 CE.[35] Pap, however, was not popular with many of the *naxarars* or the Armenian church because of his pro-Arian policy, which caused him to be slandered by the Armenian sources as devoted to the *dews* "demons" and also due to his mother's religious beliefs (Queen P'aranjem of Siwnik').[36] Pap became a victim of internal divisions and fighting among *naxarars* and the *sparapet* Mušeł Mamikonean was eventually killed at the instigation of Emperor Valens.[37] Arme-

---

[35] Garsoïan, *op. cit.*, 1997, pp. 90-91.

[36] Epic Histories IV.xliv.

[37] Garsoïan, *op. cit.*, 1997, p. 91.

nia was then divided between Šābuhr II and Valens in 377 CE and a state of relative peace reigned in the Caucasus.

Internally, a Zoroastrian priest named Adurbād ī Mahrspandān was to canonize the *Avesta* and the Zoroastrian tradition. As R.N. Frye has stated, the semblance of the Ottoman *millet* system was first begun during this period, where the Christian bishop resided at Ctesiphon and, along with the Jewish *exilarch*, paid his poll-tax in return for peace and security. By this time religious communities were being established and the foundation of a Late Antique society in Iran was being laid by the Zoroastrian priests, the Jewish rabbis, and the Christian clergy.[38] We do not know how far Šābuhr II was able to cut the power of the grandees and the clergy, but as a strong ruler he was able to affirm his will. The only hint suggesting that the Zoroastrian clergy were successful in imposing themselves on the monarchy is the fact that Šābuhr II is one of the last kings to call himself "whose lineage (is) from the Gods." It may be that finally the king of kings had become a secular ruler with minimal religious authority.

It is exactly at this juncture in history that the Sasanian monuments disappear in Persis and instead appear in the north - in Media. We may suppose that the Zoroastrian priests in Persis had become too powerful, forcing the king of kings to shift his focus not only away from their traditional stronghold, but to another place where a new image was to be presented. It is not clear what motivated this move by the king, or the adoption of the new titles.

---

[38] R.N. Frye, "Iran under the Sasanians," *The Cambridge History of Iran*, vol. 3(1), ed. E. Yarshater, Cambridge University Press, Massachusetts, 1983, p. 132.

Ardaxšīr II and Šābuhr III at Tāq-e Bustān

The artistic style is essentially different from those in Persis. Mithra's image becomes prominent, along with Ohrmazd. Ardaxšīr II (379-383 CE) and Šābuhr III (383-388 CE), successors of Šābuhr II, are presented motionless and standing frontally at Tāq-e Bustān, flanked by two small Middle Persian inscriptions bearing the traditional formulae that Ardaxšīr I had first adopted on his coins and inscriptions.[39] It seems that they are no more receiving a diadem from the gods, rather posing for a personal portrait. These kings along with Wahrām IV (388-399 CE)[40] all met a violent ends, suggesting the growing power of the nobility and the priests since the time of Šābuhr II.[41] This growing power is also reflected in the brief description of Ardaxšīr II's rule that is said to have killed a number of the great men and holders of authority in order to reduce their

---

[39] M. Back, pp. 490-491.

[40] The building of Kermānšah is associated with Wahrām IV, Th. Nöldeke, *Geschichte der Perser und Araber zur Zeit der Sasaniden*, Leiden, 1879, p. 102, ff. 2.

[41] Tabarī has Ardaxšīr II killing many of the grandees and the nobility; Šābuhr III is killed by the same noble families (Arabic *ahl al-buyūtāt*), and Wahrām IV is killed by an unnamed group, Nöldeke, 1879, pp. 100-103 which were probably by the court and nobility or the army.

power.[42] Ardaxšīr II was the younger brother of Šābuhr II and was allowed to rule by making an oath that once Šābuhr II's son (Šābuhr III) reached the age of adulthood, he would relinquish the throne. He commemorated his career with a relief at Tāq-e Bustān, standing besides Šābuhr II who is handing him the diadem of rulership. Behind Ardaxšīr II stands the deity Mihr, the god of oath and treaty. The relief corroborates Tabarī and Ferdowsī's report that Ardaxšīr II had taken an oath before Šābuhr II.

Tāq-e Bustān Relief

The figure lying beneath the feet of Ardaxšīr II has been identified as the Roman emperor Julian (the Apostate).[43] The reason for which Ardaxšīr II chose to present himself as the vanquisher of Julian may be that during the time of Julian's invasion in 363 CE, Ardaxšīr II was the king of Adiabene. This means that he took part in the battle against Julian and may have been instrumental in the war.[44]

---

[42] Tabarī, 1999, pp. 68-69.
[43] K. Erdmann, *Die Kunst Irans zur Zeit der Sasaniden*, Mainz, 1969, p. 138.
[44] A.Sh. Shahbazi, "Ardašīr II," *Encyclopaedia Iranica*, Vol. II, p. 376.

During the reign of Wahrām IV (388-399 CE), who succeeded his father Šābuhr III, Armenia lost any appearance
of independence. Its western part was integrated into the
Roman empire and the eastern part was put under the rule
of the king of kings' brother, Wahrām Šābuhr (Armenian
Vramshapuh) as king of Persarmenia in 394 CE. But
Wahrām IV's greatest achievement was his halting of the
onslaught of the Huns who had entered Syria and northern Mesopotamia at this time.[45]

The fourth century CE can be described as the time
when Christianity was seen as a major threat to Zoroastrianism and a break from the ancient tradition by the Armenians. By adopting Christianity, Armenia and then
Georgia began to become closer to the (Eastern) Roman
empire. In time the Roman emperors saw themselves as
the leaders of all Christians, rendering the Christians of the
Sasanian empire suspects in the Iranian world. A strong
king such as Šābuhr II and a Zoroastrian priest like
Adurbād ī Mahrspandān reacted to the expansion of
Christianity. This tactic was not to be fruitful, and in the
fifth century CE another way was found to appease the
situation. A strong and long-reigning king like Šābuhr II
brought stability to the Sasanian empire and secured its
borders in the west and the south. Šābuhr II's raids into the
Arabian Peninsula and the coast was not only to punish
the Arab tribes, but also to secure the Persian Gulf region.
The Sasanians could now call the Persian Gulf as their *mare
nostrum* "our sea." In the east it appears that Šābuhr II was
able to control the encroachment of the various nomadic
tribes such as the Huns and Kidarites and to create a loose
alliance with them. The institution of kingship, however,
was to be redefined as the Zoroastrian ecclesiastical hie-

---

[45] Nöldeke, p. 103, ff.1.

rarchy strengthened. From this point on, the king of kings was not known to be from the lineage of the gods (*yazdān*) anymore, but rather a secular ruler who continued to be a Mazda worshipper.

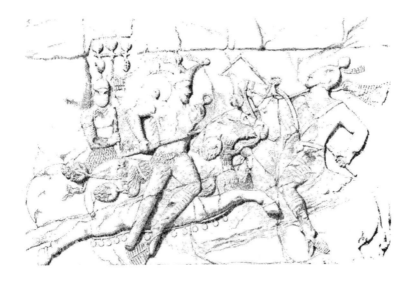

Wahrām IV

VI

Yazdgerd the Prince of Peace and the Fabled Kings in the Fifth Century

With the reign of Yazdgerd I (399-420 CE) we begin to get a new ideological outlook and treatment of the minorities in the empire. His coins have the slogan "(he) who maintains peace in his dominion" (*rāmšahr*) while the Sasanian sources called him "sinner" (Arabic *al-athīm*; Persian *bazehkar*). This seems to be purely a priestly propaganda, as he not only killed some Zoroastrian priests who had looked down upon his good treatment of the religious minorities, but also treated the Jews and the Christians favorably.[1] In fact Christianity became a recognized religion, the first synod of the "Nestorian Church" convening in 410 CE, during the rule of Yazdgerd I.[2] Agathis calls Yazdgerd I a pro-Christian monarch, but more importantly a "friendly and peaceable,"

---

[1] For Maruthas' mission to Persia and Yazdgerd's killing of some Zoroastrian priests see Socrates Scholasticus, Chapter VIII.7.9.

[2] Labourt, *Le Christianisme dans l'empire perse*, pp. 87-109; Asmussen, "Christians in Iran," *The Cambridge History of Iran*, ed. E. Yarshater, Vol. 3(2), 1983, p. 940

ruler who never made war on the Romans.[3] So, although his title would be fitting for the period, we might connect this to Kayānid ideology as well. In the Middle Persian epic, the *Ayādgār ī Zarērān* (The Testament of Zarēr) the last Kayānid ruler, Kay Wištāsp is given the title *rāmšahr* which appears in the *Dēnkard* as well.[4] This title suggests gravitation towards an Avestan / Kayānid ideology even before such titles and terminology as *kay* "Kayānid" and *xwarrah* "Glory" became prominent. How much of this new ideological framework is due to the contacts with the East is difficult to say, but the ever increasing attention paid to the eastern boundaries of the empire must have impacted the views held about the king.

By all accounts, the rule of Yazdgerd I was peaceful and mutually respectful with the Romans. This is probably best demonstrated by the fact that the emperor Arcadius (383-408 CE) asked the Persian ruler to become the guardian of his son Theodosius II.[5] This tradition lived on, the Roman and the Persian emperors occasionally asking the other for the guardianship of their heirs. By the fifth century both empires saw each other as equals and worthy to have their heirs at the court of the other, or simply securing succession and being more fearful of internal opposition than each other's forces. We should not forget that the three

---

[3] Agathias Scholasticus, *The Histories*, Book IV.26.8. For Yazdgerd I see, T. Daryaee, "History, Epic, and Numismatics: On the Title of Yazdgerd I (Rāmšahr)," *The American Journal of Numismatic*, vol. 14, 2002(2003), pp. 89-95.

A. Cameron, "Agathias on the Sassanians," *Dumberton Oaks Papers*, vol. 22-23, 1969-1970, pp. 126-127.

[4] B. Gheiby, *Ayādgār ī Zarērān*, Pahlavi Literature Series, Nemudar Publication, Bielefeld, 1999, p. 21(64); for its occurrence in the *Dēnkard* (*DkM*, 600.12) see M. Shaki, "Observations on the Ayādgār ī Zarrēn," *Archiv Orientálni*, vol. 54, 1986, p. 265.

[5] Procopius, I.ii.1-10.

kings preceding Yazdgerd I had met a violent death by the nobility. So, Yazdgerd I had to react and that he did by killing many of the aristocrats, earning the epitaph "the sinner" in the official Sasanian records. This title may be as much for his tolerance of other religions, opening a new chapter in the history of Christianity in Iran, as establishing a balance of power between the institutions of kingship, aristocracy, and the Zoroastrian clergy.

Following the death of Yazdgerd I, his eldest son, Šābuhr (Wahrām Šābuhr / Armenian *Vramshapuh*) left Armenia to take the throne but was murdered by the nobility. Instead, Xusrō, who was not directly related to Yazdgerd, was put on the throne. This action suggests the nobility and the priests' distaste for Yazdgerd I and what he had done. At the same time, his sons were put in a situation of danger. However, another son of Yazdgerd I, Wahrām, who had been sent to the Arab court at al-Hira came with a force of mainly Arabs and forced Xusrō to abdicate in 420-421 CE. By all accounts Wahrām V Gūr (420-438 CE) was a successful warrior. In 422 CE on the western front a peace treaty was signed giving religious freedom to the Christians in the Sasanian empire and to the Zoroastrians in the Roman empire. This was in the face of the persecution of Christians, instigated by the Zoroastrian priests, which seems to have begun at the end of Yazdgerd I's reign,[6] or more probably in the beginning of Wahrām's reign.[7] Wahrām defeated the Hephthalites, another invading tribe in the east, killing their king and stopping their encroachment on the eastern borders of the empire. While on his

---

[6] Cyril of Scythopolis, *Vit. Euthym* 10 (18.5-19.9) in G. Greatrex and S.N.C. Lieu, *The Roman Easter Frontier and the Persian Wars*, Part II (AD 363-630), Routledge, London and New York, 2002, p. 37.

[7] Conf. Peroz (AMS IV.258-259); Socrates Scholasticus *HE* VII.18 (363.2-365.24), Greatrex and Lieu, pp. 38-39.

campaign, it appears he had left Narsē, the youngest of his brothers, in charge. Upon Wahrām's return, Narsē was appointed the ruler of Xwarāsān on the eastern borders of the empire. We also hear of the office of *wuzurg-framādār* which was given to Mihr-Narseh.[8] Armenia's status also changed when the Armenian *naxarars* once again sought the aid of the Sasanians in deposing their king, Artašes, the son of Vramshapuh. In 428 CE, Wahrām V removed him and placed a margrave (*marzbān*) in Armenia, ushering in what is known in the Armenian history as the *marzpanate* period.

There are many romantic accounts attributed to Wahrām V, such as the immigration of Indian minstrels as entertainers (*lurs*), and his taste for drinking and especially hunting, receiving the epithet of *Gur* "onager." In the early Persian literary compendiums, the composition of the first Persian poem is also attributed to him. But this imagination he captured even by his mysterious death, where it is said that one day while hunting in Media (Māh) he fell into some marshes or a well and disappeared, his body never found. He may also be remembered by the composers of the Zoroastrian apocalyptic texts as the one who brought about an age of peace, when evil and the demons went into hiding.[9]

In the early years of the rule of Yazdgerd II (438-457 CE), the son of Wahrām V, the focus of the empire shifted to the east and to battling what the sources call "the Kušāns," probably the Huns. Yazdgerd was stationed in Xwarāsān for some time until he was able to secure the eastern flank of the empire, at the same time bringing Bactria / Balkh under the control of the Sasanians. He then

---

[8] Nöldeke, p. 136.

[9] *Zand ī Wahman Yasn: A Zoroastrian Apocalypse*, edited and translated by C. Cereti, Istituto Italiano per il medio ed Estremo Oriente, 1995, p. 152.

moved towards Armenia and Albania, as the defense of the Caucasus from the Huns moving westward was imperative, a campaign which also involved the Romans.[10] There were further problems in Armenia, probably at the instigation of Mihr-Narseh (*wuzurg-framādār* / Armenian *vzurk hramatar*), who issued an edict in which Zoroastrianism was re-imposed as the official religion in Armenia.[11] This edict provides us with an interesting glimpse of the Zurvanite[12] tendency of Mihr-Narseh and the reasons why the Armenians were required to convert back to Zoroastrianism.[13] This caused an uprising by some of the Armenian *naxarar*s who had become Christian. We can tell that the Armenians were not united in this action and as a result at the battle of Avarair in 451 CE, the Armenian forces, led by Vardan of the Mamikonian's family were annihilated, and many were deported to Iran.[14] This calamity was not to be forgotten by the Armenian (Christian)

---

[10] Priscus, frg. 41.1.1-3-27, Greatrex and Lieu, p. 57.

[11] For the inscription of Mihr-Narseh see, Back., p. 498; L. Bier, "Notes on Mihr Narseh's Bridge near Firuzabad," *Archäologische Mitteilungen aus Iran*, Vol. 19, 1986, pp. 263-268; for Mihr-Narseh's commitment to Zoroastrianism and service to fire-temples, namely those of Ardāwahišt and Abzōn-Ardaxšir see *Madigān ī Hazār Dādestān*, edited and translated by A. Perikhanian, *The Book of a Thousand Judgments*, Mazda Publishers, Costa Mesa, 1997, A39.11-17; A40.3-5.

[12] Zurvanism is somewhat different from the Orthodox Zoroastrianism in that Zurvān or the god of time becomes the father of both Ohrmazd and Ahreman, see R.C. Zaehner, *Zurvan, A Zoroastrian Dilemma*, New York, 1972.

[13] Ełishē, *History of Vardan and the Armenian War*, Translated and Commentary by Robert W. Thomson, Harvard University Press, Cambridge, Massachusetts, 1982, pp. 77-80. *The History of Łazar P'arpets'i* also covers these events, translated and commentary by Robert W. Thomson, Occasional Papers and Proceedings. Columbia University, Program in Armenian Studies, Georgia, 1991.

[14] Ełishē, pp. 178-179.

people and became a symbol of resistance towards their Zoroastrian neighbors.

The anti-Christian measures did not only befall the Armenian Christians, as there are Syriac martyrologies from this period which mention persecution of Christians and Jews. Consequently Yazdgerd II is remembered well by the Zoroastrian priests and the Sasanian chronicle as someone who defeated his enemies (non-Zoroastrians) but who behaved benevolently towards the Zoroastrians and the army. However, Yazdgerd II also sent a *marzbān* of Armenian descent by the name of Aršakān / Aršagān to Armenia and instructed him to allow the Armenians to freely practice their religion and not to further disturb them.[15] We can see this unique relationship with Armenia in the title of the "Commander of the army of the masters of the house of Armenia" (*gund ī kadag-xwadāyān-framādār ī armin*)."[16] No other region had such an office or position in the Sasanian empire.

In terms of imperial ideology, Yazdgerd II is the first to use the new title of "Mazdaean Majesty Kay" (*mzdysn bgy kdy*). This means the Sasanian kings were not seen to be in the image of the gods anymore, at least in the empire where these coins were circulated, but were connected with the Avestan dynasty of the Kayānids. However, we should remember that this trend had begun with Yazdgerd I and the title of *rāmšahr*, and that *kay* was the second manifestation of this Kayānid ideology.

It is especially interesting that this Avestan orientation takes place at the exact time when a Sasanian king is concerned again with the east and when the king resided in that region for several years. We cannot say that his stay in

---

[15] N. Garsoïan, "Frontier-Frontiers? Transcaucasia and Eastern Anatolia in the Pre-Islamic Period," *La Persia e bisanzio*, Roma, 2004, p. 347.

[16] Gyselen, 2007, p. 44.

Xwarāsān or contact with Bactria / Balkh would have brought about this fascination with the Kayānids, since we have the *rāmšahr* title appearing before. However, the Kayānid identity, which was now to be adopted wholesale by the Sasanians was to manifest itself in several titles which will be dealt with below. What is meant by "Kayānid ideology" is that rather than looking to the Achaemenids as their ancestors (for all we know they might have seen the Achaemenid monuments as the work of the kings of Persis), the Sasanians now connected themselves to the primordial and legendary kings, especially the Kayānid rulers of the *Avesta*.[17]

The two sons of Yazdgerd II, Hormizd III (457-459 CE) and Pērōz (459-484 CE) ruled consecutively, the latter deposing the former in a power struggle. According to Tabarī, Homrizd III was the elder son and ruled over Sīstān. His younger brother, however, rose in rebellion against him and a dynastic squabble lead to the rule of their mother, Queen Dēnag. Armenian sources here come to our aid, deciphering Tabarī and other Sasanian based historians. Ełīše states that the *dāyag* (mentor, governor) of Pērōz aided the young man by defeating the elder son of Yazdgerd II and putting him to death.[18] During this confusion, Albania gained independence and the eastern boarders of the empire were laid open to Hephthalite attack.

When Pērōz came to the throne, he pacified Albania, but allowed the Armenians and the Albanians to practice Christianity and made an agreement with the eastern Roman empire to cooperate in defending the passes of Cau-

---

[17] T. Daryaee, "National History or Keyanid History? The Nature of Sasanid Zoroastrian Historiography," *Iranian Studies*, vol. 28, nos. 3-4, 1995, pp. 129-141.
[18] Ełīše, p. 242; A.Sh. Shahbazi, "Hormizd III," *Encyclopaedia Iranica*, Vol. XII, pp. 465-6.

casus. The Sasanians met their match against the Hephthalites in Xwarāsān and in 469 CE. Pērōz and his harem and
retinue were captured by Xwašnawāz, the Hephthalite
leader. This took place during the third major battle, while
during the first two, the war was partly financed by the
Romans.[19] This was the low point of the Sasanian rule,
where they in fact became tributaries to the Hephthalites
and ceded territory to them in exchange for the return of
the king and his entourage. The chief priest (*mowbed*),
Pērōz's son, Kawād, and his daughter were kept with the
Hephthalites as guarantees.[20] The only reason that the
Romans did not seize the opportunity to attack Iran at this
time was the presence of internal problems faced by Emperor Zeno.[21]

---

[19] *The Chronicle of Pseudo- Joshua the Stylite*, Translated with note and
introduction by F. Trombley and J.W. Watt, Liverpool University, Press,
2000, pp. 9-10.

[20] T. Daryaee, "Ardašīr Mowbed-e Mowbedān: Yek Tashih dar Matn-e
Bundahiš," *Iranshenasi*, 2001, pp. 145-146.

[21] For the fifth century relations see Dignas and Winter, pp. 54-57; *The
Chronicle of Joshua the Stylite*, pp. 9-10.

We know there were religious persecutions, especially against the Jews, at this time and that drought and famine were rampant in the empire. A revolt in Armenia in 482 CE[22] also threatened the Sasanian dominion over its territory. Nonetheless, Pērōz had decided to revenge his loss in the east. As a result, in 484 CE, his actions cost him his life and that of seven of his sons, and his entire army.[23] It is at this juncture that we hear of the famous legend of the "pearl earring" of Pērōz, so precious that before dying he threw it to the ground so that no one could wear it.[24] Perhaps the pearl symbolically represents the sovereignty over Ērānšahr. Even if the king of kings had fallen, the empire had not. The short rule of Walāxš (484-488 CE), brother of Pērōz, was uneventful and since the empire was weak, the king kept peaceful relations with Armenia and the Hephthalites by giving tributes to the latter. Walāxš appears to have been dominated by the noble families and it is interesting to see the increasing influence of the Arsacid noble house at this time. This is exemplified by Zarmihr Sokhrā of the Karen clan who saved the rest of the Sasanian army after Pērōz's death, and also by the presence of Šābuhr of the Mehrān clan.[25] Walāxš was then deposed by the nobility and the priests in 488 CE, when Kawād I (488-496, 498-531 CE) was brought to the throne.

The fifth century kings were generally weak and the nobility and the Zoroastrian clergy were able to exert their influence at the cost of court. Some kings like Yazdgerd I did try to reduce the power of the Zoroastrian priests and

---

[22] Łazar P'arpets'i, 136.

[23] Sebeos reports that seven of Pērōz's sons were killed with him, Chapter 8.67, p. 5.

[24] For Pērōz's campaign in the east see Procopius, *History of the Wars*, Book I.i-iv.

[25] Nöldeke, p. 151, ff. 1.

the nobility, but this only hampered their eventual take-over of the Sasanian state for a short time. This, however, did not mean that the empire was not centralized or was ineffective. The bureaucratic apparatus, under the control of the priests, had reached such levels of sophistication that the death of a king could not bring the empire down, something that worked to the advantage of the priests and the nobility. This centralization is also apparent from the growing number of titles as they appear on administrative seals,[26] as well as the appearance of mint-marks on the coins. Economically, the empire was not faring well, due to the drought, famine and the incisive wars with large reparations paid to the Hephthalite, and there also was no victory in the west to collect gold from the Romans. Iran needed a strong ruler and it soon found it in the sixth century CE.

---

[26] For a detailed study of the administrative seals and the functionaries see R. Gyselen, *La geographie administrative de l'Empire sassanides*, Paris, 1989.

VII

Kawād I and Xusrō I:
Revolution and Renovation in
the Sixth Century

Kawād I had to face economic and political problems that confronted the empire at the end of the fifth century. It is at this time that we gain some information on Zoroastrian sectarianism in the Sasanian empire. In the first period of Kawād's rule, a Zoroastrian priest by the name of Mazdak was able to capture the attention of Kawād I, encouraging him to bring about reforms which went beyond the accepted religious dogma and the established social order. Mazdak brought a social reform that caused much resentment from the Zoroastrian priests during and especially after its success. Sources tell us that Mazdak preached an egalitarian social system, one in which equality in sharing wealth, women and property was propagated. Roman sources state that it was Kawād who introduced Iranians to "communal intercourse with their women."[1] Mazdak's outlook had theological and

---

[1] Procopius, *History of the Wars*, Book I.v.1-2. Also Agathias, *The Histories*, "He was even reputed to have made a law that wives should be held in common," Book 4.7, p. 130.

cosmological dimensions, but it also had political and social ramifications.[2] One needs to see the Mazdakite movement in terms of its function as a political tool for Kawād.
Using Mazdak's ideas, Kawād was able to weaken the
power of the nobility and the grandees, the large land
owners and the priests who now were involved in every
aspect of the state.[3] Mazdak's teaching, presenting a novel
interpretation of the Zoroastrian tradition, went against
the social division which was enforced by the *Avesta*, or
perhaps how the Zoroastrian priests had interpreted the
Avesta. Kawād may or may not have believed in his message, but he certainly used it to his advantage, in leveling
the upper classes and making the king more appealing and
accessible to the masses by adopting Mazdakite ideas. Imperial granaries were given away and land was redistri-
buted among the peasants. In the Zoroastrian texts composed by the very priests who were against this reform,
this period is seen as a time of chaos where women were
shared by all, and no one knew one's lineage anymore.

In 496 CE, the disgruntled nobility and the priests had
Kawād arrested and imprisoned in the "Prison of Oblivion" and brought his brother Zāmāsp to the throne.
Zāmāsp is noted for his gentleness and sense of justice
which may in fact be anti-Mazdakite propaganda.[4] He
probably attempted to undue Kawād's reforms. Kawād,
with the help of his sister, was able to escape to the Heph-

---

[2] H. Gaube in his essay has suggested that Mazdak was a fictional character, "Mazdak: Historical Reality or Invention?," *Studia Iranica*, vol. 11,
1982, pp. 111-122.

[3] P. Crone, "Kavād's Heresy and Mazdak's Revolt," *Iran*, vol. 29, 1992,
p. 30. On an ostracon found at Erk-kala from Turkmenia it is written:
"He gave a doubtful oath, but a *mowbed* should not tell lies, and he
died..." A.B. Nititin, "Middle Persian Ostraca from South Turkmenistan," *East and West*, vol. 42, no. 1, 1992, pp. 105-106.

[4] Agathias, *The Histories*, Book 4.28, p. 131.

thalites. There he raised a force and was able to recapture his throne in 499 CE, Zāmāsp abdicating in his favor. This action also demonstrated the beleaguered situation of the empire, where in a time of chaos a small force was able to overrun the nobility-priest alliance. In the first quarter of the sixth century, Kawād not only forced the Mazdakite religion on the population of the empire - where many, especially the lower classes, must have been happy - but also upon the clients of the Sasanians, such as the Arabs in Najd and Hijaz.[5] This would suggest that the developments in the Sasanian empire affected the region as well.

Once the economic, political and social situation was under control, Kawād began to institute reforms that were fundamental to the empire in the sixth century and are usually credited to his son, Xusrō I. The office of the "Protector of the Poor and Judge" *(drīyōšān jādaggōw ud dādwar)* was created from the ranks of the *mowbeds* (chief priests) to help the poor and the downtrodden which was not only a reaction to the Mazdakite movement, but a general trend in Christianity, Zoroastrianism, and later Islam.[6] Administratively, four chanceries *(dīwāns)* were created for the empire, probably corresponding to the military division of the empire under the rule of four generals *(spāhbeds)*.[7] Prior to this, an *Ērān-spāhbed* led the army, but now it had become exceedingly difficult to be on several fronts at once. The four *spāhbeds* then held sway over the quarters

[5] M.J. Kister, "Al-Hīra, Some notes on its relations with Arabia," *Arabica*, vol. xi, 1967, pp. 143-169.

[6] M. Shaki, "An Appraisal of Encyclopaedia Iranica, Vols. II and III,"*Archiv Orientálni*, Vol. 59, p. 406; and a review of the evidence T. Daryaee, "Modafe' Darvīšān va Dāvar dar Zamān-e Sāsānīān," *Tafazzolī Memorial Volume*, ed. A. Ashraf Sadeghi, Sokhan Publishers, Tehran, 2001, pp. 179-188.

[7] F. Gurnet, "Deux notes à propos du monnayage de Xusrō II," *Revue belge de Numismatique*, 140, 1994, pp. 36-37.

(*kusts*) of the empire whose names and titles we now have from the discovered seals and sealing, thanks to the work of R. Gyselen.[8]

The quadripartition was a reaction to the incursions from the east by the Hephthalites, as well as the Roman frontier wars in the west, and the Arab raids into the empire from the south. This made it crucial for the empire to be able to deal with problems on several fronts. Here we have a division of four quarters, much like the divisions in the later Eastern Roman empire, where there were *Praefectura praetorio per Orientem* "prefecture of the East;" *Praefectura praetorio per Illyricum* "prefecture of Greece and the Balkans;" *Praefectura praetorio Illyrici, Italiae et Africae* "prefecture of Illyrium, Italy and Latin Africa;" and *Praefectura praetorio Galliarum* "prefecture of Roman Britain and the Iberian Peninsula."[9]

The survey of agricultural lands and reorganization of the tax system also began during his rule, as was the creation of new districts in the empire.[10] Religiously, Nestorian Christianity became the officially tolerated church in Iran and by the time of Xusrō I we are told that the leader of the Christians had the title of *Ērān Catholicos*.[11]

Fortunately for the Sasanians, the Hephthalites were in demise by 515 CE. In the West, however, things were different; there was a protracted war beginning in 502 CE,

---

[8] R. Gyselen, *The Four Generals of the Sasanian Empire: Some Sigillographic Evidence*, Roma, 2001; for a catalogue of the seals see Gyselen, 2007, pp. 47-52.

[9] G. Ostrogorsky, *History of the Byzantine State*, Rutgers University Press, Revised Edition, New Brunswick, New Jersey, 1969, pp. 97-98; J. F. Haldon, *Byzantium in the Seventh Century*, Cambridge, 1990, p. 35.

[10] Z. Rubin, "The Reforms of Khusrō Anūshirwān," in *The Byzantine and Early Islamic Near East, States, Resources and Armies*, vol. III, ed. A. Cameron, Princeton, 1995, pp. 227-296.

[11] Sebeos, Chapter 9.70, p. 10.

ending a long period of peace. Procopius informs us that Kawād owed money to the Hephthalites,[12] while another source suggests that the Iranians were unhappy because the Romans had been unwilling to help in the defense against the Huns.[13] Kawād successfully invaded Armenia and took Theodosiopolis and Martyropolis. From Armenia he moved westward and laid siege to Amida in Mesopotamia and was able to take it over.[14] Kawād made further incursions westward, but was only partially successful in his predatory invasions in search of booty. The negotiations, however, paid off for the Iranians and in 506 CE a peace was concluded. In 524, the Iberian king Gourgenes sided with the Romans, because Kawād was trying to impose Zoroastrianism on his subjects. This threatened the Sasanian control over that kingdom but the Iranians were able to restore the area to their firm control by 528 CE. Mesopotamia was the theatre for much of the battles, beginning in 527 CE, which involved even the Arab tribes and the Huns. Nu'man III, the Sasanian vassal and the ruler of Hira, along with his Arab army was entrusted with attacking the Roman possessions in Mesopotamia. By 529 CE, as Justinian was just beginning to take control of the Eastern Roman empire, the negotiations broke down and in 530 CE Kawād invaded Dara. Justinian's capable general Belisarius was sent to defend the Roman possession against the Persian general Mehrān.[15] There were further campaigns in Mesopotamian-Syrian border as well as in Armenia, Georgia, and Lazica in 531, but none had a clear winner.[16]

---

[12] Procopius, 1.7.1.

[13] Zachariah of Mytilene. *HE* VII.3 (22.15-22), Greatrex and Lieu, p. 63.

[14] Theophanes A.M. 5996 (145.24-146.15), Greatrex and Lieu, p. 67.

[15] Procopius, I.14.34-55, Greatrex and Lieu, pp. 89-91.

[16] For these wars see G. Greatrex, *Rome and Persia at war: 502-532*, Leeds, 1998.

Arab armies of Mundhir, meanwhile, continued to fight on the side of the Sasanians, limiting the Roman army in its southern maneuvers.

We can argue that at this time, a "Sasanian political revival" was taking place, materialized in the increased control of Georgia as well as parts of inner Arabia and Oman by the Sasanians.[17] The political control also manifested itself in the movement of Sasanian subjects around the known world. Iranians had already settled in Central Asia and traders had gone to India, China, as far away as Indonesia.[18] They were more interested in business and wanted to control the trade in spices and silk, motivated by economic gain, rather than as a state sponsored activity. This increased political influence of the Sasanian state, initiated under Kawād I, also continued to progress under his successors. However, when Kawād passed away in 531 CE, the Mazdakites supported his eldest son Kāwūs (another Kayānid name along with his father). However, we know that the court and the religious hierarchy decided in favor of Xusrō I, who was younger, but also an anti-Mazdakite. It appears that Kawād had also chosen Xusrō I to be his heir.[19] Kāwūs who ruled in the north, in Tabarestān, battled Xusrō I over the control of the throne, but was ultimately defeated.[20]

---

[17] J.C. Wilkinson, "The Julanda of Oman," *The Journal of Oman Studies,* vol. I, 1975, pp. 98-99.

[18] E.H. Schafer, "Iranian Merchants in T'ang Dynasty Tales," *University of California Publications in Semitic Philology,* vol. 11, 1951, pp. 403-422.

[19] Procopius 1.21.20-22; Malalas, 18.68, p. 274.

[20] For information on Kāwūs and his discontent with Xusrō's attempt to seize the throne see Z. Mara'šī, *Tārīkh-e Tabarestān va Rōyān va Māzandarān,* ed. B. Dorn, *Geschichte von Tabristan, Rujan und Masanderan,* St. Petersburg, 1850, reprint Gostareh Publishers, Tehran, 1363, pp. 201-206.

Consequently, Xusrō I became instrumental in the murder of Mazdak and a large number of his followers who had felt secure enough to proclaim their allegiance to Mazdak openly. Although the *Šāhnāme* (*Book of Kings*) may be exaggerating the end of the Mazdakites, it has captured the imagination of the Iranians to this day in describing his end: "Kasrā (Xusrō) owned an estate with high walls. He ordered holes to be dug there and had the followers of Mazdak implanted, heads in the ground and feet upwards."[21] He then is said to have told Mazdak to enter the garden of the estate to view the seeds that he had sown and had born fruit, and when the *mowbed* (here referring to Mazdak) saw his followers in such a state he cried aloud and fell to the ground. He was then hung up and killed by volleys of arrows. At the end of the story, Ferdowsī (composer of the *Šāhnāme*) proclaims: "If you are wise, do not follow the path of Mazdak,"[22] possibly reflecting the success of Xusrō's campaign against the Mazdakites, and continuing centuries after and reflecting even in Ferdowsī's time.

Xusrō I (531-579 CE) represents the epitome of the philosopher-king in the Sasanian and Near Eastern history. There is so much that has been attributed to him that it is quite difficult to discern fact from fiction. But he certainly was able to remain in the memory of the people even after the fall of the Sasanians and the coming of Islam. Xusrō I's reforms and changes to the empire were to become a blueprint for kings, caliphs and sultans alike. To this end, Xusrō I essentially followed his father's administrative and economic reforms. But before undertaking major reforms, he needed to secure his power on the throne by limiting the power of the great noble houses. He also presented

---

[21] *Šāhnāme*, translated by R. Levy, p. 321.
[22] *Šāhnāme*, p. 321.

himself as the anti-Mazdakite candidate, reminiscing to a time when there was stability and social order. In reality, however, Xusrō I was creating a new order after the defeat and the destruction of the old one.

When Xusrō I came to power as an anti-Mazdakite, he did not restore the power of the great noble houses and the large landed aristocracy; instead he favored the small landholding gentry known in the Middle Persian and Perso-Arabic sources as *dehgāns / dehghāns*.[23] The *dehgāns* would not only be the backbone of the Sasanian military, but more importantly the economic foundation of the state as tax collectors. They would also remain as the repository of Persian culture and Iranian history for time to come, up to the eleventh century, when one of them in his poor economic state completed the *Šāhnāme* or the *Book of Kings*.

To secure the borders of the Sasanian empire, Xusrō built a series of defensive walls (*war*), similar to Hadrian's Wall of the Roman empire and the Great Wall of China. The Persian walls, however, were built on the borders of the four sides of the empire. One was built in the northeast, along the Gurgān plain to defend against the Hephthelites, one in the northwest at the Caucasus passes along the fortification at Darial (*qal'at Bāb al-Lān*),[24] one in the southeast, and reinforcing the one called the "wall of the Arabs" (*war ī tāzīgān*), in southwestern Iran.[25]

Intellectually, there seems to have been an opening of relations and exchange of ideas with other people, espe-

---

[23] For the function of the *dehgāns* see A. Tafazzolī, *Sasanian Society*, Bibliotheca Persica Press, New York, 2000, pp. 38-58.

[24] A. Alemany, "Sixth Century Alania: Between Byzantium, Sasanian Iran and the Turkic World," *Ērān ud Anērān: Studies Presented to Boris Il'ič Maršak on the Occasion of His 70th Birthday*, eds. M. Compareti, P. Raffetta, G. Scarcia, Venice, 2006, pp. 44-45.

[25] Frye, "The Sasanian System of Walls for Defense," pp. 7-15.

cially Indians and Romans. Works on medicine, astrono-
my, mirrors for princes, fables and stories, and manuals for
games such as chess were brought and translated from India.[26] From Rome, musical instruments, various scientific
works, medical treatises, and philosophical texts were
translated. Some philosophers came to the court of Xusrō I
from Athens, especially after the closing down of the
school of Neo-Platonist by Justinian. Xusrō I's interest in
philosophy is gained by noting that he was called "Plato's
Philosopher King."[27] Tolerance of the Jews and Christians
was also a feature of Xusrō I's rule. Indeed, the Catholicos
or the head of the Christian church in the East was the bishop of Seleucia-Ctesiphon.[28]

Xusrō's palace at Ctesiphon

In a sense, Xusrō I and the Roman Emperor Justinian
represented the enlightened monarchs and memorable ru-

[26] T. Daryaee, "Mind, Body, and the Cosmos: The Game of Chess and
Backgammon in Ancient Persia," *Iranian Studies*, vol. 34, no. 4, 2002, pp.
281-312.

[27] Agathias actually portrays Xusrō's encounter with the philosophers
quite negatively, *The Histories*, Book 2.3. For a judicious and corrective
view to Agathias see J.Th. Walker, "The Limits of Late Antiquity: Philosophy between Rome and Iran," *Ancient World*, vol. 33, 2002, pp. 45-
69.

[28] J.Th. Walker, *The Legacy of Mesopotamia in Late Antique Iraq: The Legend
of Mar Qardagh the Assyrian*, Berkeley and Los Angeles, 2007, p. 92.

lers of Late Antiquity. Their sense of being just (NP. *ādel*), as Persian texts refer to Xusrō I, their efforts in codification of laws, (the text *Madyān ī Hazār Dādestān*, probably begun in the time of Xusrō I, as well as *Codex Justinianus*), and administrative and military reforms which took place almost simultaneously in both empires point to the lasting effects of both emperors on their empires. Scholars argue whether one king influenced the other, but rather than trying to see the process one way, one can view the relations as reciprocal, where each challenged and perhaps wanted to outdo the other.

Xusrō I completed the administrative and military reforms of his father. This was the division of the empire into four regions, placing a general *spāhbed* in each quadrant. He also instituted a registry or *dīwān* for the military. He drew on different tribal people such as the Daylamites to enforce the military which in time led to a different military composition whose loyalty lay with the king. There was also tax reforms, where taxes were excised not only based on the size of the land, but on the type of produce.

With these reforms, Xusrō I was able to reinvigorate the Sasanian empire and their effectiveness can be gleaned from his military successes. In the east, in 557-558 CE, Xusrō I defeated the Hephthalites and between 572 to 577 CE, checked Turkic incursions into the Near East.[29] In the west, Xusrō I concluded a treaty with Justinian, favorable to the Iranians, which came to be known as "The Eternal

[29] On the Persian military tactics and capabilities see *Maurice's Strategikon*, Handbook of Byzantine Military Strategy, Translated by G.T. Dennis, University of Pennsylvania Press, Philadelphia, 1984, pp. 113-115. Also for the Iranian material see A. Tafazzolī, "Un chapitre du Dēnkard sur les guerriers," *Au carrefour des religions: Mélanges offerts á Philippe Gignoux*, Res Orientales VII, Peeters, Leuven, 1995, pp. 297-302. An old but useful treatment of Persian military tactics is by K. Inostrantsev, *Motal'ātī darbare-ye Sāsānīān*, BTNK, Tehran, 1348, pp. 49-89.

Peace" in 532 CE. The Iranians received gold to protect the Caucasus pass, retained control over most of Armenia and Iberia and the Romans agreed to relinquish their bases in Mesopotamia.[30] In 540 CE, however, Xusrō I began a campaign in the West, encouraged by the Gothic king Vitiges who informed of Justinian's campaigning in North Africa and Italy, and the Armenian pleas for help from the Iranians.[31] Xusrō I started his campaign in Mesopotamia and Syria, where the city of Antioch was taken.[32] There was another campaign in 542 CE, but a plague dissuaded the king from going further, but the warfare resumed in 543 CE when the Romans were defeated in Armenia, and in 544 the Iranians laid siege to Edessa, exacting a large amount of gold from its inhabitants. In 540 CE at the instigation of the Armenians and the Lazics, Xusrō I again invaded Armenia to reduce Roman harassment in the region. This war proved to be a long one, beginning in 541 and lasting until 557 CE when a truce was agreed upon. Then Xusrō I took to the eastern borders of his empire, waging war on the Hephthalites and defeating them, hence controlling the lands up to the Oxus.

This latest truce lasted until 565 CE when Justinian passed away. Justin II, who became the new emperor, demanded the control over Suania.[33] This became a cause for war, one that proved disastrous for the Romans and by 573 CE Iranians made substantial gains in the Caucasus, Mesopotamia and Syria. Dara was again taken by Xusrō I, a

---

[30] Greatrex and Lieu, pp. 96-97.

[31] Procopius, II.2-3.

[32] Malalas 18.87 (405.65-479.23-480.5), and other notices Greatrex and Lieu, pp. 103-107.

[33] Theophanes (of Byzantium) 1 (*FHG* IV.270), Greatrex and Lieu, 2002, pp. 135-136.

major blow to position of the already ill Justin II.[34] With the new emperor, Tiberius, there were negotiations over Mesopotamia but the fighting continued in the Caucasus in 574-575 CE and then in Mesopotamia. This stage of warfare lasted intermittently all through the reign of Emperor Maurice and beyond, until the seventh century.[35] Such cities as Dara and Apamea were conquered and their population were taken to the Sasanian territory. The numbers were in hundreds of thousands; according to the Syriac Chronicle of 846, some 98,000 from Dara were taken and according to John of Ephesus, 292,000 from Apamea.[36] According to M. Morony, the deportations were due to the labor shortage caused by drought, famine, disease and warfare, and the Sasanians need to repopulate these regions.[37]

Xusrō's son, Hormizd IV (579-590 CE) came to the throne when his father was attempting to make lasting peace between Rome and Iran. He had chosen Hormizd IV as heir to the throne for similar reasons. Although the exact genealogy of Hormizd IV is not clear, it is for certain that on his mother's side, he was related to the Turks. Hormizd IV's mother was probably the daughter of the king of the Xazars.[38] If this is so, it means that Xusrō I wanted to also secure the Darband pass where the Xazars ruled and at times threatened the empire. In most sources Hormizd is noted for his arrogance, tyranny and making

---

[34] Theophanes (Byzantium) 4 (FHG IV.271), Greatrex and Lieu, 2002, p. 150.

[35] For the sixth century relations see Dignas and Winter, 2007, pp. 57-65.

[36] M. Morony, "Population Transfers between Sasanian Iran and the Byzantine Empire," *La Persia e bisanzio*, Roma, 2004, p. 175.

[37] *Ibid.*, p. 179.

[38] On Hormizd's maternal genealogy see A.Sh. Shahbazi, "Hormozd IV," *Encyclopaedia Iranica*, , Vol. XII, pp. 466-467

many enemies at the court.[39] Sebeos tells us that Hormizd IV was responsible for the killing of many of the nobility, which must have made him much hated.[40] He continued his support of the landed gentry or *dehgān*s who probably grew in strength at the cost of the nobility (*āzādān*) and dealt harshly with the Zoroastrian priests as well. These sources should not necessarily persuade us that Hormizd was an evil ruler. Rather, he was probably trying to continue his father's work in reducing the power of the nobility and as is the usual case in Sasanian historiography, he was seen as harsh, brute and evil. This slander becomes clear when we read that he was unwilling to persecute the Christians, despite a petition made by the Zoroastrian priests.[41]

Hormizd's negotiations with the Romans were less successful and caused a long and costly war. Tiberius was willing to cede Armenia to the Sasanians and exchange outposts in Arzenere for Dārā.[42] With the collapse of the negotiations, the Roman general Maurice invaded Iran all the way to Media,[43] and another army laid siege to Ctesiphon. The Sasanians countered them in Mesopotamia and defeated the Romans in Armenia.[44] In 581 CE Maurice was forced to go back to Constantinople to take the throne, but his army kept on fighting and even when Hormizd IV suggested peace, the Romans did not accept the invitation.[45]

---

[39] Theophylact Simocatta, Book iii.17.1

[40] Sebeos, Chapter 10.73, p. 14.

[41] Tabarī, 1999, pp. 297-298.

[42] Theophylact Simocatta, Book iii.17.1-3.

[43] Theophylact Simocatta, Book iii.17.4.

[44] Menander Protector, p. 217.

[45] For details of the events see Theophylact Simocatta, Book i.1.1-15.

To make matters worse, in 589 CE, the Hephthalites invaded Eastern Iran. They were met by the Sasanian general Wahrām Čōbīn whose victory over them made the general famous within the empire. He was from the noble Arsacid family of Mihrān and could trace his genealogy further back than the Sasanians. After minor defeat in Armenia against the Romans, Hormizd IV slandered Wahrām Čōbīn and made false accusations against him, causing the general to rebel and move towards Ctesiphon.[46] With the help of the nobility, led by Hormizd's brothers-in-law Wīstahm and Wīndōe, they deposed the king and brought his son, Xusrō II (Parwēz)to power.[47]

These events took place in 589-590 CE and it was quite important that it was the first time that someone outside the family of Sāsān had attempted to take over the empire, probably a shock to the Sasanian family.[48] This may characterize the strength of the centralized system and the problems with the Sasanian imperial propaganda, especially when a weak or hated king was on the throne. The institutions which were reformed and strengthened during the time of Kawād I and Xusrō I were so powerful and entrenched by this time that they functioned regardless of the political chaos. The same may be said of the local affairs, where the *dehgāns* became the important officials and local matters became more important for the local population than the political affairs of the empire. One can suggest that when further damage was done to the Sasanian im-

---

[46] Theophylact Simocatta, Book iv.1.1.

[47] For details of the events see A. Sh. Shahbazi "Hormozd IV," *Encyclopaedia Iranica*, , Vol. XII, pp. 466-67.

[48] For the effect of the Arsacids on the downfall of the Sasanians see the very important work of P. Pourshariati, *Decline and Fall of the Sasanian Empire: The Sasanian-Parthian Confederacy and the Arab Conquest of Iran*, IB Tauris, (forthcoming 2008).

perial propaganda in the seventh century and the Arab Muslim conquest, it did not really shake up the institutions and officials of the empire. In fact the "system" continued to function under Muslim governors. This is evidenced by the adoption of the Persian administrative system and its employees by the Caliphate.

VIII

From Xusrō II to Yazdgerd III: The Pinnacle and Fall of the Sasanian Empire

At the time of his father's death, Xusrō II Abarwēz (NP. Parvīz) was at Partaw, ruling over the realm or camp of Albania (*Šahr-Ālānyōzān*)[1] as king of Albania (*Alān-šāh*).[2] He was not able to withstand the forces of Wahrām Čōbīn[3] and did not feel safe within the empire, fleeing to the Eastern Roman empire in 590 CE and taking refuge in the city of Hierapolis where he sought the aid of the Emperor Maurice.[4] The Roman emperor supplied Roman and mainly Armenian forces to Xusrō II, which enabled him to come back to the empire that same year and defeat Wahrām. The now renegade general took

---

[1] For the identification of this name on the papyri see D. Weber, "Ein bisher unbekannter Titel aus spätsassanidischer Zeit?," *Corolla Iranica. Paperes in honour of Prof. D.N. MacKenzie on the occasion of his 65ᵗʰ birthday*, Frankfurt, 1991, pp. 228-235.

[2] Alemany, p. 46.

[3] Theophylact Simocatta, Book iv.9-10.

[4] Theophylact Simocatta, Book iv.12.8. For a different version of the content of the letter sent by Xusrō to Maurice see Sebeos, Chapter 11.76, pp. 18-19.

to the east and was eventually assassinated at the instigation of Xusrō II by the Turks. We know that Wahrām considered himself a legitimate king, since he minted coins for
two years (590-591 CE), in the first year in the southwest,
primary in Mesopotamia and Media and then in the
second year in the northeast where he had fled. Regardless
of his death, Wahrām remained in the imagination of the
people who composed songs and stories about him that
survived in Arabic and Persian.

Xusrō II

When Xusrō II came to the throne, he began to take revenge on those who had a hand in the murder of his father, although we are not sure if he himself was innocent
of the crime. His uncle Wīstahm, who had been his sup-
porter, was targeted and as a result took to Media, minted
coins in his own name and probably lived there until 600
CE.[5] So in the last decade of the sixth century, two people
who were not deemed to be the legitimate rulers by the

---

[5] It is known that he has coins with the year 6, but Paruck states that he
had also seen a year 10 coin which may be correct, since every time
Xusrō II defeated his enemies, changes took place on his coins, see T.
Daryaee, "Religio-Political Propaganda on the Coins of Xusro II," *American Journal of Numismatics*, vol. 7, 1997, pp. 141-154

Sasanians minted coins. This is significant, since in 366 years, no one except the Sasanian king was allowed or was able to mint coins in his own name. It is with this damage to the Sasanian prestige and to the family of Sāsān that we may turn to Xusrō II's conquests.

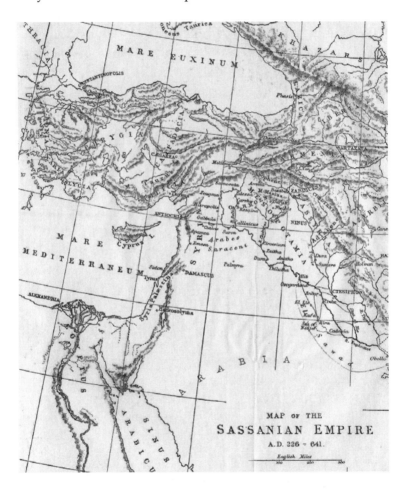

MAP OF THE
SASSANIAN EMPIRE
A.D. 226 - 641.
English Miles

Xusrō II consolidated his power around the Persian Gulf and sent envoys to Arabia, as far as Mecca to inquire about the situation. When the last king of Hira, Nu'man III ibn al-Mundir was killed, the Lakhmid state was put under Iranian loyalists in 602 CE. When the Roman emperor, Maurice was removed and Phokas came to the throne, Xusrō II used this event as a pretext for the conquest of Syria and beyond. At first, Roman Armenia was captured by Xusrō II,[6] and in 604 CE with blazing speed, his two generals Šāhīn and Šahrwarāz conquered Syria.[7] Palestine in 614 CE and then Egypt were taken in 619 CE, and the Iranians even went as far as Libya,[8] while Anatolia was conquered between 619-622 CE. We have vivid descriptions by Antiochus Strategos of the conquest of the city of Jerusalem in 614 CE and the taking of the holy cross which resonated in the Roman empire which condemned it strongly.[9] We should remind ourselves that this is an early Christian view of things. The Jewish sources provide us with a more nuanced view of the events in Jerusalem. A Piyyutim or Jewish liturgical poem from the period suggests that the Jews initially saw the Iranians as their savior. Indeed the Sasanians allowed the Jews not only to inhabit the city (against the already existing Roman ordinance), but also to build an altar and reoccupy the Jewish sacred spaces.[10] But

---

[6] *Narratio de rebus Armeniae*, 109-13 (p. 41), Greatrex and Lieu, pp. 186-187.

[7] M. Morony, "Syria Under the Persians 610-629," *Proceedings of the Second Symposium on the History of Bilād al-Shām During the Early Islamic Period up to 40 A.H. / 640 A.D.*, ed. M.A. Bakhit, Amman, 1987, pp. 87-95.

[8] R. Altheim-Stiehl, "The Sasanians in Egypt - Some Evidence of Historical Interest," *Bulletin de la société d'archéologie Copte*, vol. 31, 1992, p. 87, 92; on the papyrological evidence see E. Venetis, "The Sassanid Occupation of Egypt (7th Cent. A.D) According to Some Pahlavi Papyri Abstracts," *Greco-Arabica*, vols. 9-10, 2004, pp. 403-412.

[9] Antiochus Strategos, in F.C. Conybeare, "Antiochus Strategos' Account of the Sack of Jerusalem in A.D. 614," in *English Historical Review*, vol. 25, 1910, pp. 502-517. Also see *Chronicon Paschale*, for the events of 614, p. 156.

[10] H. Sivan, "Palestine between Byzantium and Persia (CE 614-618)," *La Persia e bisanzio*, Roma, 2004, p. 90.

by 618 CE the balance of favor had tipped towards the Christians.[11] We know that Xusrō II was not anti-Christian. In fact he had already presided over the election of a new patriarch of the Church of the East in 605 CE, a sign of royal favor.[12]

Because of his spectacular victories and achievements, Xusrō II minted such legends on his especial issue coinage as "Iranians have become fearless" (*ērān abē-bēm kard*), and "Iranians became strong" (*ērān abzōnhēnēd*).[13] This is the Sasanian empire at the apex of its glory and power, headed by a heroic king.

Gold coin of Xusrō II

The conquest of Jerusalem shocked the Eastern Roman empire and its new emperor, Heraclius (610 CE).[14] Heraclius was intent on leaving for North Africa, but it is said that his mind was changed by the clergy and with the aid of church funds, mounted a counterattack. From the Black Sea he entered Armenia and went into the heart of the Sasanian empire in 624 CE, sacking the sacred Adur Gušnasp

[11] *Ibid., p. 91.*

[12] Walker, 2007, p. 87.

[13] These coins may be his and not that of Xusrō II if we are to accept *Bundahišn*'s account, bestowing these titles to Xusrō I.

[14] For events in Byzantium see A.N. Stratos, *Byzantium in the Seventh Century*, Vol. I, Amsterdam, 1968.

temple at Shiz [15] in retaliation for the taking of the "True Cross" by the Sasanains. The first real crusade between the Christian world and the East (Zoroastrian) had taken place and the Arab Muslims had not even begun their conquest. Along with the retreating Iranian army, the Persian nobility and those attached to the Persians also retreated from Syria and Mesopotamia.[16] In matter of years, Xusrō II went from a world conqueror, emulating the Achaemenid territorial integrity, to a humiliated king who was unable to protect the sacred Zoroastrian fire-temples and his population. Xusrō II was removed in 628 CE by the nobility and the priests, and all the conquered territories were returned to the Romans by 630 CE.[17] What was different in this campaign is that Xusrō II had gone beyond the norm and had made deep incursions in the heart of the Eastern Roman empire, destabilizing it and as J. Howard-Johnston has said "destroying the long-established binary world order."[18] This change would haunt both empires, destroying one and amputating major territories of the other.

---

[15] Theophanes A.M. 6114, 307.19-308.25; Movsēs Daskhuranst'i II.10 (130.3-132.5), Greatrex and Lieu, pp. 200-203, and for other sources see N. Garsoïan, "Byzantium and the Sasanians," *The Cambridge History of Iran*, ed. E. Yarshater, Vol. 3(1), Cambridge University Press, 1983, p. 592.

[16] J.M. Fiey, "The Last Byzantine Campaign into Persia and Its Influence on the Attitude of the Local Populations Towards the Muslim Conquerors 7-16 H. / 628 A.D.," *Proceedings of the Second Symposium on the History of Bilād al-Shām During the Early Islamic Period up to 40 A.H. / 640 A.D.*, ed. M.A. Bakhit, Amman, 1987, p. 97.

[17] Some sources state that Xusrō II had fallen ill in Ctesiphon and was dying, Theophanes A.M. 6118 (325.10-327.16), Greatrex and Lieu, 2002, p. 223.

[18] J. Howard-Johnston, "Pride and Fall: Khusro II and His Regime, 626-628," *La Persia e bisanzio*, Roma, 2004, p. 113.

Xusrō II between Anāhīd and Ohrmazd

In terms of imperial ideology, while the early Sasanians considered themselves to be from the lineage of gods, they also used Persian Achaemenid titles, such as "King of Kings" on their coins and inscriptions. This heritage was set aside by the adoption of the Kayānid ideology from the fourth to the sixth century CE. However, Xusrō II proclaimed a return to the dual heritage of the Achaemenid and Kayānid ideology by minting coins in his name with the title of "King of Kings" and also inscribing for the first time the slogan, "increased in glory" (*xwarrah abazūd*). *Xwarrah* is central to the ancient Iranian royal ideology as demonstrated in the *Avesta*, and is a prerequisite for rulership in the Iranian world. In Iranian art this glory was shown usually with a halo around the king's head.[19]

---

[19] For the latest study see A. Soudavar, *The Aura of the Kings: Legitimacy and Divine Sanction in Iranian Kingship*, Mazda Publishers, Costa Mesa, 2003.

Xusrō II was a warrior-king, in style of the kings of the early Sasanian period. His grotto at Tāq-e Bustān shows him in full armor, characteristic of the Sasanian heavy cavalry, and shows the deity Anāhīd, the Lady of Waters, above him. In many ways Xusrō II represents the culmination of Sasanian absolutism and a return to the past glories for one last time. While Ohrmazd was held to be supreme, at Tāq-e Bustān one also encounters two other deities, namely Mihr (Mithra) and Anāhīd (Anahītā). These are the triple deities that were mentioned by Artaxerxes II in the Achaemenid period; this seems to be a full return to devotion to these deities. The lavishness of the court of Xusrō II is clearly demonstrated by the Tāq-e Bustān rock-reliefs, where the king is shown on a boat, hunting, and musicians playing their harps, along with the courtly retinue. Xusrō II has gone down in Iranian history as an opulent[20] king who brought ruin to the Sasanian empire. But perhaps his religious policy, specifically his interest in Christianity was a source of his condemnation by the Zoroastrian sources.[21] His favorite wife, Šērīn is well known in the epic and romance literature, and is said to have propagated Christianity in the empire,[22] along with his other Christian wife Maryam who was an Eastern Roman princess.

After Xusrō II, Kawād II (Šērōe) came to the throne in 628 CE. His reign started with a series of fratricides, killing almost every eligible or capable male heir from the Sasanian family. This again may have been due to the fact that

---

[20] There are illusions to his opulence in the a short Middle Persian text, *Māh Frawardīn Rōz ī Hordād*, passage 27, translated by S. Kiyā, where eighteen amazing things were beheld by Xusrō.

[21] According to Sebeos, Chapter 46.149, p. 115 after the capture of Jerusalem, Xusrō assembled the Christian bishops in his court and presided over their disputation.

[22] Sebeos, Chapter 13.85, p. 29.

Xusrō II had previously crowned a younger brother of Kawād, named Mardānšāh, as his heir. However, Kawād's actions would come to have devastating effects on the future of the empire. He did not want to be associated with his father's memory, a fact apparent from his coinage which reverted to the style of Xusrō I.[23] In 629 CE, Kawād II, made a peace treaty with Heraclius in which he returned all the lands previously held by the Romans.[24] The Persian general Šahrwarāz met the Roman emperor at Arabissus Tripotamus, where Euphrates was set as the permanent boundary between the Sasanian and the Roman empires.[25] Shortly afterwards, Kawād II was himself assassinated like his brothers which exposed the beleaguered state of royal affairs at Ctesiphon.

In 630 CE, Kawād's young son, Ardaxšīr III, came to the throne and it was during his reign that for a third time the Sasanian family was challenged by an outsider. This time it was Šahrwarāz, the Sasanian general who had led the armies of Xusrō II, who entered the capital at Ctesiphon and put an end to the rule of the young king and proclaimed himself the new king of kings. His actions may have been partly as a result of his respect for Xusrō II, since he punished and killed all those who had a hand in the murder of the fallen king. His peace with Heraclius in 629 CE and probably the latter's backing, according to one Armenian source, gave Šahrwarāz the impetus to conquer and take over the throne.[26] This again was a serious set-

---

[23] For a treatment of Kawād II and his career see H.M. Malek, "The Coinage of the Sasanian King Kavād II (AD 628)," *The Numismatic Chronicle*, vol. 155, 1995, pp. 119-129.

[24] *Chronicon anyonymum ad a.d. 1234 pertinens*, 100, Greatrex and Lieu, p. 225.

[25] *Chronicon 724*, 147.18-24, Greatrex and Lieu, p. 226.

[26] Sebeos, Chapter 40.129, p. 88.

back to the Sasanian imperial ideology. However, Šahrwarāz was not able to secure his throne and in a matter of months he too was killed.[27]

This time, one of the daughters of Xusrō II, named Bōrān, came to the throne in 630 CE and ruled for two years.[28] Her rule was a period of consolidation of the imperial power and the rebuilding of the empire. She attempted to unite the empire and relieve the population of heavy taxes, as the Islamic sources report. Her notions of the past and respect for her father are also clear, as she reverted her coinage type to that of her father. She also minted gold coins which were ceremonial in nature and were not meant for wide circulation, suggesting that she was the restorer of her lineage, *i.e.*, the race of gods which was emphasized in the early Sasanian period. The legend on her coin reads: "Bōrān, restorer of the race of Gods" (*bōrān ī yazdān tōhm winārdār*).[29] Of course something should be said of a woman assuming the throne in the Sasanian empire. She was probably installed on the throne, since she was the only legitimate heir (along with her sister) who could rule, as Kawād II had murdered all of her brothers.[30] She also attempted to keep good relations with

---

[27] *Chronicle of Seert* 93, PO 13.556, Greatrex and Lieu, *op. cit.*, p. 227.

[28] H.M. Malek & V. Sarkhosh Curtis, "History and Coinage of the Sasanian Queen Bōrān (AD 629-631)," *The Numismatic Chronicle*, vol. 158, 1998, pp. 113-129.

[29] T. Daryaee, "The Coinage of Queen Bōrān and its Significance in Sasanian Imperial Ideology," *Bulletin of the Asia Institute*, vol. 13, 1999, pp. 77-83.

[30] For a detailed study of Queen Bōrān see H. Emrani, *The Political Life of Queen Bōrān: Her Rise to Power and Factors that Legitimized her Rule*, MA Thesis, California State University, Fullerton, 2005.

the Romans and sent the *Catholicos* Mar Isho-Yab to Heraclius and so had the opportunity to reorganize the empire.[31]

Bōrān was, however, deposed by another Sasanian general and here we see that the military generals are more frequently assuming power in the face of the shaken institution of kingship, the competing nobility and the Zoroastrian priests. Soon after, Queen Azarmī(g)duxt ruled for a brief period, and her coins have the bust of a man, probably a reuse of the older coins, not having enough time to mint new coins. Between 632 CE when Bōrān died and when Yazdgerd III assumed the throne, there were a number of "contender-kings" who assumed the throne and were either removed or were challenged by other distant members of the family of Sāsān. This period may be called a period of factionalism and division within the empire. We have a list of kings who struck coins and others who are known only from the literary sources, but this era is confusing in terms of succession and only a tentative sequence of the rulers can be supplied. The list is as follows: Jošnasbandah, Azarmī(g)duxt, Hormizd V, Xusrō III, Pērōz II, and Xusrō IV.[32] The late Sasanian empire was beginning to resemble the Arsacid feudal system before the fall of the Arsacids. This system left the local officials and *dehgāns* as the most powerful elite, since the rulers and governors were not able to hold power.[33] From the numismatic evidence it appears that Hormizd V, Xusrō III,

---

[31] For the seventh century relations see Dignas and Winter, pp. 67-71; *The Khuzistan Chronicle*, 29, Greatrex and Lieu, p. 237.

[32] For this period in Sasanian history see, T. Daryaee, *Fall of the Sasanian Empire and the end of Late Antiquity: Continuity and Change in the Province of Persis*, Ph.D. Thesis, UCLA, 1999.

[33] For the importance of the *dehqāns* in the late Sasanian and early Islamic period see, A. Tafazzolī, *Sasanian Society*, Ehsan Yarshater Distinguished Lecture Series, Bibliotheca Persica Press, New York, 2000, pp. 38-58.

Pērōz II and Xusrō IV ruled different areas of the empire simultaneously from the end of 631 CE to 637 CE, when Yazdgerd III had already been on the throne for some years.[34] Hormizd V has been identified as Farrox-Hormizd, the General who may have had a hand in the death of Āzarmī(g)duxt.[35] He was a powerful king as he minted coins in Xūzestān and Persis (Fārs).[36] Xusrō III appears to have been a child who was raised by one faction to kingship at the same time in the province of Kermān.[37]

Thus we can see that during this period, some power resided at the capital at Ctesiphon where the king was crowned, and in the provinces, the *dehgāns* working with the local Zoroastrian priests, ruled the different regions of the empire. Then there were individuals in the provinces who also claimed kingship, far away from Ctesiphon. Yazdgerd III himself was crowned at the Anhāhīd fire-temple at Istakhr in 632 CE, the old center of power for the family of Sāsān. This might be significant not only symbolically but also in relation to the region that was still loyal to the Sasanian family, providing a safe harbor for the young king of kings. His rule, however, coincided with the Arab Muslim invasion of the Near East and the Eastern Mediterranean.

---

[34] For a chronology of events and rulers see T. Daryaee, *Soghūt-e Sāsāniān (The Fall of Sasanians)*, Nashr-e Tarīkh-e Irān, 2004, pp. 59-79.

[35] M.I. Mochiri, *Études de numismatique Iranienne sous les Sassanides*, Tome I, Téhéran, 1972, pp. 13-16.

[36] For the coinage and mints see R. Gyselen, *New Evidence for Sasanian Numismatics: The Collection of Ahmad Saeedi*, Res Orientalis XVI, Bures-sur-Yvette, 2004, p. 66.

[37] Mochiri, p. 17; Gyselen, *ibid.*, p. 66.

Coin of Yazdgerd III

Yazdgerd III was forced to move from province to province demanding loyalty, money and support. During his rule, Iran resembled the medieval Germanic system of rule, *i.e.,* a Wandering Kingship. Between 629 and 630 CE Arab Muslims were able to wrest Yemen and Bahrain from the Sasanians and convert its Iranian ruler and population to Islam. Those Arab and Iranians in Oman, Yemen and Bahrain who chose to remain Zoroastrian were allowed to do so by paying tribute. In 632 CE when the prophet Muhammad passed away, the Zoroastrians in Oman rebelled and an Arab Muslim army was sent to pacify them.

In 633 CE the Muslim armies made important gains by entering southern Mesopotamia (Iraq). Khaled ibn Walīd was able to conquer the Sasanian client kingdom of Hira, destroying the buffer between the Sasanians and the Arabs in the desert. This was not entirely due to Arab Muslim power, since Xusrō II himself had initiated the downfall of Hira when he deposed and killed the powerful king of the Lakhmids upon his attempt at independence. At the battle of D'āt al-Salasel in 633 CE the frontier forces under the leadership of Hormoz / Hormizd were defeated by the Muslim army. Although the Iranian general was able to receive reinforcement, he was again defeated by Khāled in Mēšān/Maysan. Khāled moved further north, defeating more Sasanian regiments. Finally by January of 634 the Sawād had become part of the Arab Muslim dominion once Khāled defeated the joint Iranian and Arab force. The impact of Khāled's activity was high enough to weaken and destroy most of the Sasanian defense fortifications, leaving the entire Mesopotamia defenseless before a stronger Arab Muslim army.

The Sasanians, however, did not sit idly by and with fresh forces defeated the Arab Muslims at the battle of the Bridge in 634 CE, by the Euphrates. In 635, another Persian general, named Mehrān ī Mehrwandād, crossed the Euphrates and attacked the Arab armies who were trying to regroup. This campaign was disastrous as Mehrān, along with many of his forces, were killed and this further left the Sawād open to the Arab Muslims. The Muslim armies then pillaged from Kaskar/Kašgar to Anbār. In 636 CE southern Mesopotamia fell completely into the hands of the Muslims as they defeated the Sasanians at the battle Maḍār.

In June 637 CE after several months of occasional face off, the major and disastrous battle of Qadisiya took place. The Arabs were reinforced just in time from Syria and the Iranian general, Rustam ī Farroxzādān, along with a large number of his soldiers, were killed in the battle. Some of the Sasanian forces now joined the Muslim forces and switched sides afterwards, taking on the conquest of the Sasanian empire. The remaining Sasanian forces fought one more battle at Bābel (Babylon) but were again defeated.

Some sources state that Ctesiphon fell to the Arab Muslims when they entered it unopposed, and this was followed by the nobility and the courtiers fleeing before them to the heart of Iran.[38] This tradition is not for sure. In fact it appears that for several months the city was besieged.

---

[38] Sebeos, Chapter 42.136, p. 98.

Sa'ad ibn Abi-Waqqās who was responsible for the victory at Qadisiya also commanded the siege and managed to break into the city. With the riches at Ctesiphon in the hands of the Muslims, they could now finance any campaign to the ends of Ērānšahr.

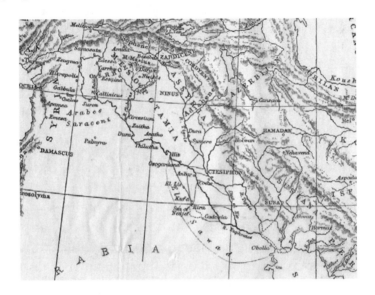

In December 637 CE the Sasanian forces under the leadership of Rustam ī Farroxzādān's brother, Khorrzad (Xwarrah-zād) fought again at the battle of Jalūlā. Those Iranians who did not die in battle were slaughtered later and their women and children captured. Yazdgerd III who had fled Ctesiphon, now headed for Ray. The Arab forces left Ctesiphon and made Kūfa their center, allowing those Iranians who agreed to pay tribute to return to the city. The fall of Mesopotamia (Iraq) to the Arab Muslims had significant ramifications for the rest of the 640s and 650s. As M. Morony has pointed out, once Ctesiphon, the administrative center of the Sasanian fell, there was disorder throughout the empire. The heart of the empire was stopped and so the rest of the body was in shock.[39] Right away, the Muslim army, somewhat helped by the Iranians, began to not only take over the chancery system of the Sasanians, but to also create a regular standing army. They could finance wars from the riches they had accumulated in Mesopotamia and specifically Ctesiphon. The Arab Muslims now not only enlisted Iranians in their forces, but also acquired military equipment that was superior to what they had before and matched those of the Sasanian army.[40] In turn, the Sasanian troops who joined the Muslims were known as (Arabic) *mawālī* or *halīf* who became professional fighters for pay.[41]

Under Umar's direction, Xūzestān fell in 642 CE and in the same year Māh (Media) was taken at the battle of Nīhāvand. The career of one of the generals of the Sasanians named Hormozān is well-known in these campaigns.[42] He was the *marzbān* of Xūzestān and in charge of the right wing of the Sasanian forces at the battle of Qadisiya. Hormozān regrouped and fought again at the battle of Jalūlā. He then fought and escaped capture in the same region, while many of his forces were killed by the Arab Muslims. He finally surrendered in 642 CE and was taken to Medina, but initially did not convert to Islam. While in Medina, he advised Caliph Umar in making important fiscal and institutional changes. He later married into the house of Ali ibn Abi-Talib (the fourth Caliph) and after the murder of Caliph Umar, was accused of involvement in the plot and then killed by the Caliph's son, Ubayd-allāh. His murder initiated a major response from Ali ibn Abi-

---

[39] M. Morony, "Arab Muslim Conquest," *Encyclopaedia Iranica*, Vol. II.

[40] *Ibid.*,

[41] M. Zakeri, *Sāsānid Soldiers in Early Muslilm Society. The Origins of 'Ayyārān and Futuwwa*, Wiesbaden, 1995, p. 113.

[42] A.Sh. Shahbazi, "Hormozān," *Encyclopaedia Iranica*, Vol. XII, pp. 460-1.

Talib who stated that Ubayd-allāh did not have any right to kill a Muslim based on accusation.[43]

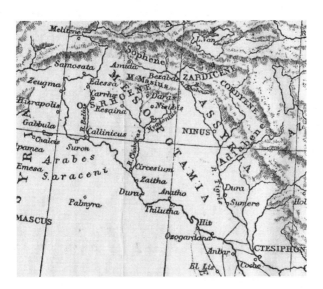

These victories laid the heart of Iran open to conquest without any major military resistance. Only the battle of Nīhāvand which took place in 642 CE is important. Under the generalship of Mardānšāh who was the son of Hormozān, a long battle, fought for several days, took place. Mardānšāh was killed and the Muslims were victorious. In the 640s the Arab Muslims took over the heartland of the Iran, conquering Hamedān, Qazvin and Ray. Adūrbadagān also had a similar fate. Each of these cities was given protection, their fire-temples undisturbed and the people were not taken into slavery, based on the terms of the capitulation treaties which demanded huge sums of tribute (Ray 500,000 and Ardebīl 100,000 drahms/dirhams). In the same time period another contingent of Muslim forces captured Isfahan and Kāšān and established them-

---

[43] Shahbazi, *ibid.*

selves at Qom. Another Arab force headed from Nīhāvand to Xūzestān and then Fārs. The Sasanians in Xūzestān put up a stiff resistance, notably by Pērōz and also the *ostāndār* (governor) of Fārs. When the Caliph Umar died in 644 CE, many cities revolted and it took until 650 CE for the Ērānšahr to be pacified again. While in the initial stage of the conquest, Mesopotamia had been devastated and pillaged, the second stage of the conquest was brutal for central Iran and Fārs. Yazdgerd III had been present in the difficult battle in Fārs where many of the Iranian soldiers perished. He now only could go to the east, towards Kermān, then Sīstān and finally to Marw in the northeast. In Kermān and Sīstān it appears that the *marzbān*s did not answer Yazdgerd's requests for reinforcement and money. The Kermānīs and Sīstānīs put up a heavy resistance against the Muslims, but were ultimately defeated. Yazdgerd III was faced with local officials who were unwilling to help him and he was defeated by a confederation of local officials, the *marzbān* of Marw and the Hephthalite ruler of Bāghdīs. Tradition has it that he was killed in 651 CE in Marw by a miller who did not recognize who king Yazdgerd was.

The Muslim victory was successful for a series of reasons. In addition to the internal problems, the heavy Sasanian cavalry was left paralyzed by the Arab light cavalry which was much more maneuverable. The Islamic texts usually report the number of the Iranian soldiers to have been in the hundreds or tens of thousands and several times larger than the Arab armies. This of course is pure fiction and it is boastful literature which aims to aggrandize Muslim achievements, which may be compared to the Greek accounts of the Greco-Persian wars. The Sasanian state would not have been able to muster such a large force against the Muslims, since many had been killed or were not present because of the long wars with the Eastern Roman empire and the internal strife.

Upon conquest, the Muslims usually gave the *marzbāns* or local rulers several choices. These included either converting and becoming part of the Islamic ocumene, or accepting Muslim rule but paying tributes to keep their freedom and practice their religion. The last choice was to resist and fight. The last choice of course meant either death or the danger of being taken into slavery, when they had to pay even more tribute for their freedom.[44] Those in charge of the cities, more often after Mesopotamia was taken, chose to conclude a treaty and accept Muslim sovereignty. This then ensured their privileges even under the Muslim rule.[45]

The sons of Yazdgerd III fled to the east asking the T'ang emperor, Gaozong, to aid them in their battle against the Arab Muslims. Pērōz, the elder son of Yazdgerd III, established a kingdom called the "Persian Area Command" (*Bosi dudufu*) stationed at Zarang between 658 and 663 CE. He was recognized as the legitimate king of Iran by the Chinese,[46] but by 674-675 CE we hear that he went to the Chinese capital, probably because of further Muslim victories.[47] He died around 679 CE and his son Narsē was placed on the throne of Iran in exile. Pērōz has been remembered by a stone statue of him, still in existence at the entrance of the mausoleum of Gaozong with the inscription: "Pērōz, King of Persia (Iran), Grand Gen-

---

[44] Zakeri, p. 105.

[45] Zakeri, p. 108.

[46] J. Harmatta, "The middle Persian-Chinese Bilingual Inscription from Hsian and the Chinese-Sāsānian Relations," *La Persia nel Medioevo*, Accademia Nazionale dei Lincei, Roma, 1971, p. 374.

[47] A. Forte, "On the Identity of Aluohan (616-710) A Persian Aristocrat at the Chinese Court," *La Persia e l'Asia Centrale da Alessandro al X secolo*, Accademia Nazionale dei Lincei, Roma, 1996, p. 190.

eral of the Right Courageous Guard and Commander-in-chief of Persia (Iran)."[48] There the family of Sāsān kept their royal status, became military generals, and had temples built at Tun-huang (sha-chou), Wu-wei (Liang-chou), Ch'ang-an (founded in 631 CE) and at Loyang and lived along other Iranians who had been there for commercial activity or had fled as a result of the Muslim conquests.[49] The other son of Yazdgerd III, Wahrām (*Aluohan* in Chinese sources) attempted to recapture the lost territories from the Arab Muslims. Although he was ultimately unsuccessful, the Middle Persian texts, especially a small apocalyptic Middle Persian poem called *Abar Madan ī Wahrām ī Warzāwand* (On the Coming of the Miraculous Wahrām), may have a kernel of truth in regard to his campaigns. He died in 710 CE.[50] Wahrām's son, Xusrō (*Juluo* in Chinese sources) who with the aid of the Turks invaded Iran, was not able to defeat the Muslims either and this is the last time we hear of someone from the family of Sāsān trying to capture the throne of Iran.[51] We can end our long narrative by retelling the poem, as Persians usually begin

---

[48] C. Guocan, "Tang Qianling shirenxiang ji qi xianming de yanjiu," *Wenwu jikan*, Vol. 2, 1980, p. 198b8; Forte, *ibid.*, p. 191.

[49] The classical work on Chinese-Persian relations in this period is that of B. Laufer, *Sino-Iranica: Chinese Contributions to the History of Civilization in Ancient Iran, with Special Reference to the History of Cultivated Plants and Products*, Field Museum of Natural History, Publication 201, Anthropological Series, vol. 15, no. 3, Chicago, 1919; also see E.H. Schafer, *The Golden Peaches of Samarkand, A Study of T'ang Exotics*, University of California Press, 1963, pp. 10-25; For a more general treatment see J. Gernet, *A History of Chinese Civilization*, Cambridge University Press, 1982, pp. 282-287. The latest work is by M. Compareti, "The Last Sasanians in China," *Eurasian Studies*, vol. II, no. 2, 2003, pp. 197-213.

[50] C. G. Cereti, "Again on Wahrām ī Warzāwand," *La Persia e l'Asia Centrale da Alessandro al X secolo*, Accademia Nazionale dei Lincei, Roma, 1996, pp. 629-639.

[51] Harmatta, p. 375; Forte, pp. 193-194.

or finish a story. The aspirations of the Iranians who saw their empire fall before the Muslims is captured in the mentioned Middle Persian poem,[52] about the son of Yazdgerd III, summing up their view of the events:

When will it be when a messenger come from India,
(to say) that King Wahrām from the lineage of the Kayanids has arrived,
that there are a thousand elephants, over their heads are elephant-
drivers,
that has an adorned flag in the manner of the renowned kings,
that will go before the army as the army leader,
a dispatch must be sent, a clever interpreter,
when he goes he would tell the Indians,
what we saw at the hand of the Arabs,
with one troop (they) weakened the religion and killed the kings,
(they have killed) our king and among those Iranians,
their religion is in the manner of the demons, they eat bread like the
dogs
they took sovereignty from the renowned kings,
not by skill, not by manliness,
but through mockery and scorn,
through oppressiveness, they took from the people,
women and sweet property, gardens and orchards,
they have placed poll-tax, divided it over the heads,
again they have sought the cloth (and) heavy tribute,
behold how much evil that demon has cast in this world,
there is no more evil than they in the world,

---

[52] There are several translation of this poem, H.W. Bailey, *Zoroastrian Problems in the ninth-century Books*, Oxford, 1948, pp. 195-196; J.C. Tavadia, "A Rhymed Ballad in Pahlavi," *Journal of the Royal Asiatic Society*, 1955, pp. 29-36; F. de Blois, "A Persian Poem Lamenting the Arab Conquest," *Studies in honour of Clifford Edmund Bosworth*, ed. C. Hillenbrand, Leiden, 2000, pp. 82-95; M.-Š. Bahar, "Yek qaside-ye Pahlavi," *Sokhan*, year 2, 1324, pp. 577-581, reprinted in *Tarjome-ye čand matn-e Pahlavi*, ed. M. Golbon, Tehran, 1347(reprint 1379), pp. 131-141; B. Gheybi, *Āmadan-e šāh bahrām-e varjāvand*, Nemudar Publishers, Bielefeld, 1372, and finally T. Daryaee, "On the Coming of a Zoroastrian Messiah: A Middle Persian Poem on History and Apocalypticism in Early Islamic Iran," *Festschrift for Amin Banani*, ed. M. Tehranian (forthcoming 2008).

among us will come that king Wahrām the miraculous from the lineage
of the Kayanids,
then we will bring revenge on the Arabs,
in the manner which Rustam brought a hundred revenge of Siyāwash,
we will destroy the mosques, establish fires,
we will raze idol-temples and blot them from the world,
till evil gets destroyed, the evil creatures from the world.

Appendix

Genealogy

Sasanian Family Tree

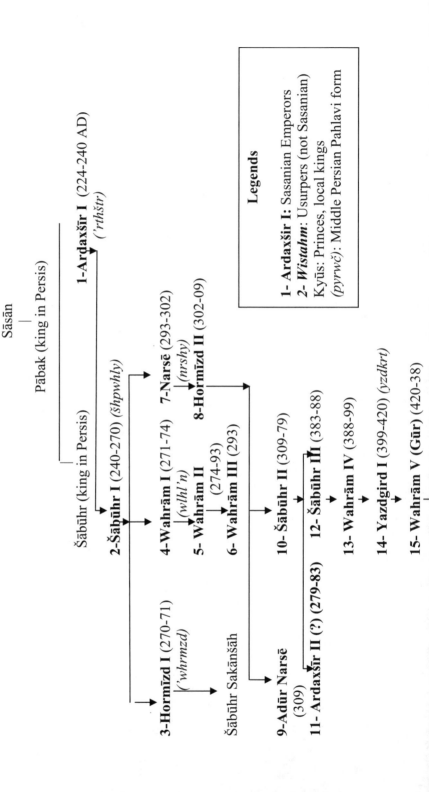

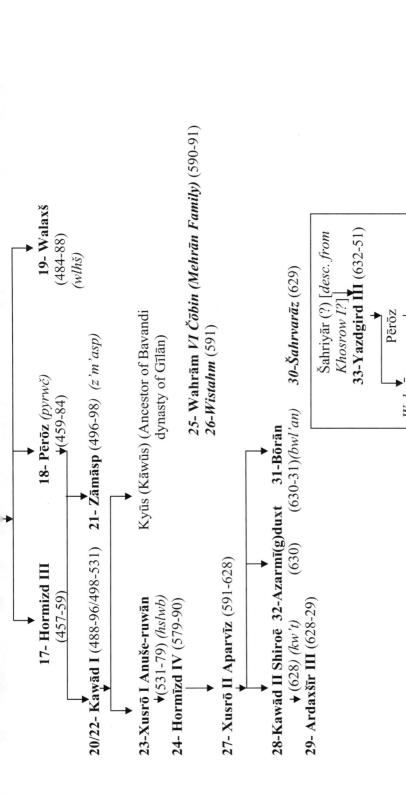

19- Walaxš (484-88) *(wlhš)*

18- Pērōz *(pyrwč)* (459-84)

17- Hormizd III (457-59)

21- Žāmāsp (496-98) *(z'm'asp)*

Kyūs (Kāwūs) (Ancestor of Bavandi dynasty of Gīlān)

25- Wahrām VI Čōbin (Mehrān Family) (590-91)

26-Wistahm (591)

30-Šahrvarāz (629)

20/22- Kawād I (488-96/498-531)

23-Xusrō I Anuše-ruwān (531-79) *(hslwb)*

24- Hormīzd IV (579-90)

27- Xusrō II Aparvīz (591-628)

31-Bōrān (630-31)*(bwl'an)*

28-Kawād II Shiroē (628) *(kw't)*

32-Azarmī(g)duxt (630)

29- Ardaxšīr III (628-29)

Šahriyār (?) *[desc. from Khosrow I?]*

33-Yazdgird III (632-51)

Wahrām

Pērōz

Narsē (died in China)

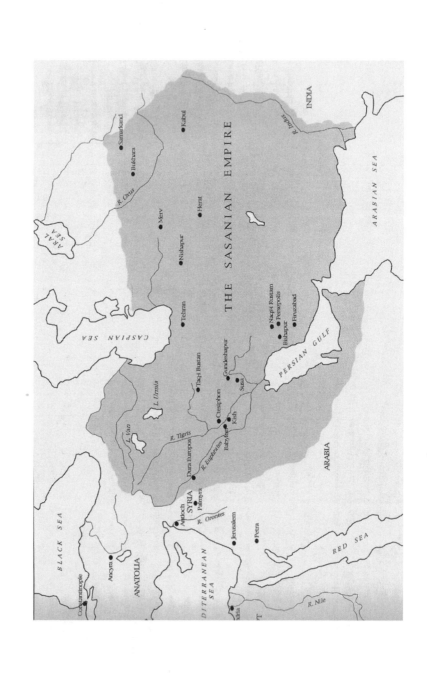

Bibliography

Primary Textual Sources

Arabic

Meskaweyh, A.A.R. *Tajarib al-umam*, Tehran, 1369.

al-Tabarī, M.J. *Ta'rīkh al-rusul wa-al-mulūk*, ed. M.J. de Goeje, Leiden, 1879-1901. The German translation by Th. Nöldeke, *Geschichte der Perser und Araber zur Zeit der Sasaniden*, Leiden, 1879; The English translation with copious notation is by C.E. Bosworth, *The History of al-Tabarī, Vol. V, The Sāsānids, the Byzantines, the Lakhmids, and Yemen*, State University of New York Press, 1999.

al-Tha'alibi, A.M.A.M.M.I. *Ghurar Axbar al-mulūk al-Fars wa Sayrhum*, ed. H. Zotenberg, Paris, 1990.

Armenian

Agathangełos, *History of the Armenians*, Translation and Commentary by R.W. Thomson, State University of New York Press, Albany, 1976.

Buzandaran Patmut'iwnk' *The Epic Histories Attributed to P'awstos Buzand*, Translated and Commentary by N. Garsoïan, Harvard University Press, 1989.

Ełishē, *History of Vardan and the Armenian War*, Translated and Commentary by R.W.Thomson, Harvard University Press, Cambridge, Massachusetts, 1982.

Łazar P'arpets'i, *The History of Łazar P'arpets'i*, Translated and Commentary by R.W. Thomson, Occasional Papers and Proceedings. Columbia University, Program in Armenian Studies, Georgia, 1991.

Sebeos, *The Armenian History attributed to Sebeos*, Translated and Notes by R.W. Thomson, Historical commentary by J. Howard-Johnston, Assistance from T. Greenwood, 2 vols., Liverpool University Press, Liverpool, 1999.

Greek & Latin

Agathias Scholasticus, *Agathias: The Histories*, translated by J.D.C. Frendo, 1975.

Ammianus Marcellinus, *The Surviving Books of the History*, edited and translated by J.C. Rolfe, Cambridge, Massachusetts, 1937-1939.

Antiochus Strategos, in F.C. Conybeare, "Antiochus Strategos' Account of the Sack of Jerusalem in A.D. 614," in *English Historical Review*, vol. 25, 1910, pp. 502-517.

Chronicon Paschale, translated by M. Whitby and M. Whitby, Liverpool University Press, 1989.

Dio Cassius, *Dio's Roman History*, translated by E. Cary, Loeb Classical, Cambridge University Press, 1969.

Herodian, translated by C.R. Whittaker, Loeb, Cambridge University Press, 1970.

Menander Protector, *The History of Menander the Guardsman*, translated by R.C. Blockley, 1986.

Procopius: History of the Wars, translated by H.B. Dewing, Loeb Classical Library, Harvard University Press, 1992.

Theophylact Simocatta, edited and translated by M. Whitby and M. Whitby, Liverpool University Press, 1986.

Middle Persian

Abar Madan ī Wahrām ī Warzāwand, edited and translated into English by M.F. Kanga, in *All India Oriental Conference,* 12, iii, pp. 687-691. Translated into Persian by S. Oriān, *Motūn-e Pahlavī,* Tehran, 1371, pp. 190-191.

Ayādgār ī Zarērān, edited and translated in German by D. Monchi-Zadeh, Uppsala, 1981. Into Persian by B. Gheiby, Pahlavi Literature Series, Nemudar Publication, Bielefeld, 1999.

Bundahiš, edited and Translated by B.T. Anklesaria, *Zand ī Akāsīh,* Bombay, 1956. In Persian by M. Bahār, *Bondahēš,* Tūs Publishers, 1369.

Dēnkard, Sanjana, *The Dēnkard,* edited and translated by D.P. Sanjana, vol. xvi, Kegan Paul, trench, Trubner & Co., London, 1917 provides a complete but outdated translation. Also E. W. West, *Pahlavi Texts,* The Sacred Books of the East, Oxford, 1880; For book 3 J.P. de Menasce, *Dēnkart III,* Paris, Librairie Klincksieck, 1974; book 5 J. Amuzegār and A. Tafazzolī, *Dēnkard V,* Cahiers de Studia Iranica, Peeters, Leuven, 2001. *Dēnkard V,* Studia Iranica – Chaier xx, 2001; book 6 Sh. Shaked, *Wisdom of the Sasanian Sages,* Caraban Books, 1979; book 7 M. Molé, *La légende de Zoroastre,* Paris, 1967.

Husraw ud Rēdag, edited and translated into English by D. Monchi-Zadeh, "Xusrōv ut Rētak," Monumentum Morgenstierne, vol. II, Acta Iranica 22, Leiden, 1982, pp. 47-91. C.J. Brunner, "Khusraw, Son of Kawad, and A Page, A Middle Iranian 'Didactic' Text," *Special Supplement to the Grapevine,* Selected Texts from Pre-Islamic Iran.

Kārnāme-ye ardašīr ī bābakān, edited and translated into English by E.K. Antia, Bombay, 1900. Into Persian by S. Hedāyat, Amir Kabir Publishers, Tehran, 1332. Also B. Farahwašī, Tehran, 1354; F. Grenet, *La Geste d'ardashir fils de pâbag, Kārnāmag ī Ardaxšīr ī* Pābagān, editions A Die, 2003.

Madigān ī Hazār Dādestān, edited and translated by A. Perikhanian, *The Book of a Thousand Judgments,* Mazda Publishers, Costa Mesa, 1997; M. Macuch, *Das sasanidische Rechtsbuch "Mātakdān i Hazār Dātistān,"* Teil II, Wiesbaden, 1981; *ibid., Rechtskasuistik und Gerichtspraxis zu Begin des siebenten Jahrhunderts in Iran,* Wiesbaden, 1993.

Šahrestānīhā ī Ērānšahr, A Catalogue of the Provincial Capitals of the Ērānšahr, J. Markwart, ed. G. Messina, Pontificio Istituto Biblico, Rome, 1931, and T. Daryaee, *Šahrestānīhā ī Ērānšahr, A Middle Persian Text on Geography, Epic and* History, Mazda Publishers, Costa Mesa, 2002.

Wizārišn Čatrang ud Nahišn Nēw-Ardaxšīr, A. Panaino, *La novella degli scacchi e della tavola reale,* Mimesis, Milano, 1999. Into English by C.J. Brunner, "The Middle Persian Explanation of Chess and Invention of Backgammon," The Journal of Ancient Near Eastern Society of Columbia University, vol. 10, 1978, pp. 45-53. T. Daryaee, "Mind, Body and the Cosmos: The Game of Chess and Backgammon in Ancient Persia," *Iranian Studies,* vol. 35, no. 4, 2002, pp. 281-312.

Zand ī Wahman Yasn: A Zoroastrian Apocalypse, edited and translated into English by C. Cereti, Istituto Italiano per il medio ed Estremo Oriente, 1995. Translated into Persian as *Zand ī Wahman Yasn,* M.T. Rashid Mohassel, Tehran, 1370.

Persian

Ibn Balxī, *Fārsnāme,* ed. Le Strange & Nicholson, Cambridge University Press, 1921.

Mara'šī Z. *Tārīkh-ē Tabarestān va Rōyān va Māzandarān,* ed. B. Dorn, *Geschichte von Tabristan, Rujan und Masanderan,* St. Petersburg, 1850, reprint Gostareh Publishers, Tehran, 1363.

Nāma-ye Tansar, ed. M. Mīnoī, Tehran, 1352. English translation by M. Boyce, *The Letter of Tansar,* Rome, 1968.

Šāhnāme, Moscow Edition, 1968 ; Dj. Khaleghi-Motlagh & M. Omidsalar, *The Shahnamah of Ferdowsi,* Vol. 6, Biblitheca Persica, 2007.

Syriac

The Chronicle of Pseudo- Joshua the Stylite, Translated with note and introduction by F. Trombley and J.W. Watt, Liverpool University, Press, 2000.

Secondary Sources

Alemany, A. "Sixth Century Alania: Between Byzantium, Sasanian Iran and the Turkic World," *Ērān ud Anērān: Studies Presented to Boris Il'ič Maršak on the Occasion of His 70th Birthday,* eds. M. Compareti, P. Raffetta, G. Scarcia, Venice, 2006, pp. 43-50.

Alram, M. *Iranische Personennamenbuch, Nomia Propria Iranica in Nummis,* vol. 4, Vienna, 1986.

_____. "The Beginning of Sasanian Coinage," *Bulletin of the Asia Institute,* vol. 13, 1999, pp. 67-76.

_____ & Gyselen, R. *Sylloge Nummorum Sasanidarum Paris –Berlin Wien,* Band I, Wien, 2003.

_____ & Gyselen, R. *Sylloge Nummorum Sasanidarum Paris –Berlin Wien,* Band II, Wien, 2003.

Altheim-Stiehl, R. "Das früheste Datum der sasanidischen Geschichte, vermittelt durch die Zeitangabe der mittelpersisch-parthischen Inschrift aus Bīšāpūr," *Archäologische Mitteilungen aus Iran*, vol. 11, 1978, pp. 113-116.

_____. "The Sasanians in Egypt - Some Evidence of Historical Interest," *Bulletin de la société d'archéologie Copte*, vol. 31, 1992, pp. 87-96.

Amin, S. *Eurocentrism*, New York, 1989.

Asmussen, J.P. "Christians in Iran," *The Cambridge History of Iran*, ed. E. Yarshater, Vol. 3(2), 1983, pp. 924-948.

Back, M. *Die Sassanidischen Staatsinschriften, Studien zur Orthographie und Phonologie des Mittelpersischen der Inschriften zusammen mit einem etymologischen Index des mittelpersischen Wortgutes und einem Textcorpus der behandelten Inschriften*, Acta Iranica 18, E.J. Brill, Leiden, 1978.

Bailey, H.W. *Zoroastrian Problems in the Ninth-Century Books*, Oxford, 1971.

Barnes, T.D. "Constantine and the Christians of Persia," *The Journal of Roman Studies*, vol. 75, 1985, pp. 126-136.

Bausani, "Two Unsuccessful Prophets: Mani and Mazdak," *Religion in Iran. From Zoroaster to Baha'ullah*, Bibliotheca Persica Press, New York, 2000, pp. 80-110.

Bayānī, Š. *Šāmgāh-e Aškāniyān va Bāmdād-e Sāsānīān*, Tehran, 2535.

Bernal, M. *The Black Athena. The Afro-asiatic Roots of Classical Civilization*, New Brunswick, N.J., 1987.

Blaut, J.M. *The Colonizers' Model of the World: Geographical Diffusionism and Eurocentric History*, Trenton, N.J., 1993.

Blockley, R.C. "Subsidies and Diplomacy: Rome and Persian in Late Antiquity," *Phoenix*, vol. 39, no. 1, 1985, pp. 62-74.

de Blois, F. "The Middle Persian Inscription from Constantinople: Sasanian or Post-Sasanian," *Studia Iranica*, vol. 19, 1990, pp. 20-16.

Bowersock, G.W. *Julian the Apostate*, Harvard University Press, Cambridge, Massachusetts, 1978.

Braudel, F. *The Perspective of the World: Civilization and Capitalism 15th-18th Century*, University of California Press, Berkeley & Los Angeles, 1992.

Briant, P. "The Seleucid Kingdom, the Achaemenid Empire and the History of the Near East in the First Millennium BC," *Religion and Religious Practice in the Seleucid Kingdom*, Aarhus, 1990, pp. 40-65.

_____. "Du Danube à l'Indus, l'histoire d'un empire," *L'Iran et la Perse, Le Monde de la bible*, No. 106, 1997, pp. 23-26.

_____. *From Cyrus to Alexander. A History of the Persian Empire*, Eisenbrauns, 2002.

Brock, S. "Christians in the Sasanian Empire: A Case of Divided Loyalties," *Studies in Church History*, vol. 18, 1982, pp. 1-19.

_____. and Harvey, S. "Persian Martyrs," *Holy Women of the Syrian Orient*, 1998.

P. Callieri, "A proposito di un'iconografia monetale dei dinasti del Fārs post-achemenide," *OCNUS*, vol. 6, 1998, pp. 25-38.

_____. "At the roots of the Sasanian royal imagery: the Persepolis graffiti," *Ērān ud Anērān: Studies Presented to Boris Il'ič Maršak on the Occasion of His 70ᵗʰ Birthday*, eds. M. Compareti, P. Raffetta, G. Scarcia, Venice, 2006, pp. 129-148.

Cameron, A. "Agathias on the Sassanians," *Dumberton Oaks Papers*, vol. 22-23, 1969-1970, pp. 67-183.

Capdetrey, L. *Le pouvoir séleucide: Territoire, administration, finances d'un royaume hellénistique (312-129 avant J.-C.)*, Presses Universitaires de Rennes, 2007.

Conybeare, F.C. "Antiochus Strategos' Account of the Sack of Jerusalem in A.D. 614," in *English Historical Review*, vol. 25, 1910, pp. 502-517.

Cereti, C.G. "Again on Wahrām ī Warzāwand," *La Persia e l'Asia Centrale da Alessandro al X secolo*, Accademia Nazionale dei Lincei, Roma, 1996, pp. 629-639.

Chaumont, M.L. "Le culte de Anāhitā à Stakhr et les premiers Sassanides," *Revue d l'Histoire des Religions*, Vol. 153, 1958, pp. 154-175.

_____. "Vestiges d'un courant ascétique dans le zoroastrisme sassanide d'apres le Vie livre du Dēnkart," *Revue de l'histoire des religions*, CLVI, no. 1, 1959, pp. 1-24.

_____. "Le culte de la déesse Anāhitā (Anahit) dans la religion des monarques d'Iran et d'Arménie au Ier siècle de notre ère," *Journal Asiatique*, Vol. 253, 1965, pp. 168-171.

_____. "Les grands rois sassanides d'Arménie (IIIéme siécle ap. J.-C.)," *Iranica Antiqua*, vol. 8, 1968, pp. 81-93.

_____. *La Christianisation de l'empire iranien des origins aux grandes persecutions du IVe siècle*, Peeters, Leuven, 1988.

Choksy, J.K. "A Sasanian Monarch, His Queen, Crown Prince and Dieties: The Coinage of Wahram II," *American Journal of Numismatics*, vol I, 1989, pp. 117-137.

Christensen, A. *L'Iran sous les sassanides*, Copenhagen, 1944.

Crone, P. "Kawād's Heresy and Mazdak's Revolt," *Iran*, vol. 29, 1991, pp. 21-42.

Daryaee, T. "National History or Keyanid History? The Nature of Sasanid Zoroastrian Historiography," *Iranian Studies*, vol. 28, nos. 3-4, 1995, pp. 129-141.

_____. "Religio-Political Propaganda on the Coins of Xusro II," *American Journal of Numismatics*, vol. 7, 1997, 141-154.

_____. "Apocalypse Now: Zoroastrian Reflections on the Early Islamic Centuries," *Medieval Encounters*, vol. 4, no. 3, 1998, pp. 188-202.

_____. "Sasanian Persia," *Iranian Studies*, vol. 31, nos. 3-4, 1998, pp. 431-462.

_____."Laghab-e Pahlavī-ye 'čihr az yazdān' va Šāhanšāhī-ye Sāsānī," *Nāme-ye Farhangestān*, Vol. 4, No. 4, 2000, pp. 28-32.

_____. "Modafe' Darvīšān va Dāvar dar Zamān-e Sāsānīān," *Tafazzolī Memorial Volume*, ed. A. Ashraf Sadeghi, Sokhan Publishers, Tehran, 2001, pp. 179-189.

_____. "Mind, Body, and the Cosmos: Chess, Backgammon in Ancient Persia," *Iranian Studies*, vol. 35, no. 4, 2002, pp. 281-312.

_____. "Ardašīr Mowbed-e Mowbedān: Yek Tashih dar Matn-e Bundahiš," *Iranshenasi*, 2002, pp. 145-147.

_____. "The Coinage of Queen Bōrān and its Significance in Sasanian Imperial Ideology," *Bulletin of the Asia Institute*, vol. 13, 1999(2002), pp. 1-6.

_____. "Memory and History: The Construction of the Past in Late Antique Persia," *Nāme-ye Irān-e Bāstān, The International Journal of Ancient Iranian Studies*, vol. 1, no. 2, 2002, pp. 1-14.

_____. "Notes on Early Sasanian Titulature," *Journal of the Society for Ancient Numismatics*, vol. 21, 2002, pp. 41-44.

_____. "History, Epic, and Numismatics: On the Title of Yazdgerd I (Rāmšahr)," *Journal of the American Numismatic Society*, vol. 14, 2002(2003), pp. 89-95.

_____. "The Ideal King in the Sasanian World: Ardaxšīr ī Pābagān or Xusrō Anōšag-ruwān?," *Nāme-ye Irān-e Bāstān, The International Journal of Ancient Iranian Studies*, vol. 3, no. 1, 2003, pp. 33-45.

_____. "Šapur II," *Encyclopaedia Iranica*, ed. E. Yarshater (forthcoming 2008).

Dignas, B. and Winter, E. *Rome and Persia in Late Antiquity. Neighbours and Rivals*, Cambridge, 2007.

Dodgeon, M. and Lieu, S.N.C. *The Eastern Roman Frontier and the Persian Wars AD 226-363*, London, 1991.

Elton, H. *Frontiers of the Roman Empire*, Indiana University Press, Bloomington and Indianapolis, 1996.

Emrani, H. *The Political Life of Queen Bōrān: Her Rise to Power and Factors that Legitimized her Rule*, MA Thesis, California State University, Fullerton, 2005.

Erdmann, K. *Die Kunst Irans zur Zeit der Sasaniden*, Mainz, 1969.

Fiey, J.M. *Communautés syriaques en Iran et Irak des origines à 1532,* London, 1979.

_____. "The Last Byzantine Campaign into Persia and Its Influence on the Attitude of the Local Populations Towards the Muslim Conquerors 7-16 H. / 628 A.D.," *Proceedings of the Second Symposium on the History of Bilād al-Shām During the Early Islamic Period up to 40 A.H. / 640 A.D.,* ed. M.A. Bakhit, Amman, 1987, p. 97-110.

Forte, A. "On the Identity of Aluohan (616-710) A Persian Aristocrat at the Chinese Court," *La Persia e l'Asia Centrale da Alessandro al X secolo,* Accademia Nazionale dei Lincei, Roma, 1996, pp. 187-197.

_____. "Edict of 638 Allowing the Diffusion of Christianity in China," in P. Pelliot, *'Inscription nesotrienne de Si-Ngan-Fou,* edited with Supplements by A. Forte, Scuola di Studi sull'Asia Orientale, Kyoto and Collège de France, Institut des Hautes Études Chionises, Paris, 1996.

Frye, R.N. "Notes on the early Sassanian State and Church," *Studi Orientalistici in onore di Giorgio Levi Della Vida,* Rome, 1956, pp. 314-335

_____. "The Persepolis Middle Persian Inscriptions from the time of Shapur II," *Acta rientalia,* vol. xxx, 1966, pp. 83-93.

_____. "Sasanian Seal Inscriptions," *Beiträge zur Alten Geschichte und deren Nachleben, Festschrift für Franz Altheim zum 6.10.1968,* eds. R. Stiehl und H.E. Stier, Zweiter Band, Walter de Gruyter & Co., Berlin, 1970, pp. 77-84.

_____. "Sassanian Clay Sealings in the Baghdad Museum," *Sumer,* Vol. 26, 1970, pp. 237-240.

_____. "Methodology in Iranian History," *Neue Methodologie in der Iranistik*, ed. R.N. Frye, Otto Harrassowitz, Wiesbaden, 1974, p. 57-69.

_____. "The Sasanian System of Walls for Defense," *Studies in Memory of Gaston Wiet*, Jerusalem, 1977, pp. 7-15.

_____. *The History of Ancient Iran*, C.H. Beck'sche Verlagsbuchhandlung, München, 1983.

_____. "The Political History of Iran Under the Sasanians," *The Cambridge History of ran*, ed. E. Yarshater, Vol. 3(1), 1983, pp. 116-180.

_____. "Zoroastrian Incest," *Orientalia Iosephi Tucci Memoriae Dicata*, eds. G. Gnoli and L. Lanciotti, Istituto Italiano per il Medio ed Estremo Oriente, Roma, 1985, pp. 445-455.

Garibolid, A. "Royal Ideological Patterns Between Seleucid and Parthian Coins: The Case of Θεοπάτωρ," *Commerce and Monetary Systems in the Ancient World: Means of Transmission and Cultural Interaction, Melammu Symposia V*, ed. R. Rollinger and Ch. Ulf with collaboration of K. Schengg, Franz Steiner Veralg, 2004, pp. 363-384.

_____. "Astral Symbology on Iranian Coinage," *East and West*, vol. 54, 2004, pp. 31-53.

_____. "Royal and Ideological Pattersn Between Seleucid and Parthian Coins: The Cast of Θεοπάτωρ," in *Commerce and Monetary Systems in the Ancient World: Means of Transmission and Cultural Interaction, Melammu Symposia V*, ed. R. Rollinger and Ch. Ulf with collaboration of K. Schnegg, Franz Steiner Verlag, 2004, pp. 366-384.

Garsoïan, N. "Protecteur des pauvres," *Revue des études arméniennes*, tome XV, 1981, pp. 20-34.

_____. "Byzantium and the Sasanians," *The Cambridge History of Iran*, ed. E. Yarshater, Vol. 3(1), Cambridge University Press, 1983, pp. 568-593.

_____. "The Marzpanate (428-652)," The Armenian People From Ancient to Modern Times, ed.R. Hovannisian, New York, 1997, pp. 95-116.

_____. "Frontier-Frontiers? Transcaucasia and Eastern Anatolia in the Pre-Islamic Period," *"La Persia e bisanzio*, Roma, 2004, pp. 327-352.

Gaube, H. "Kavād's Heresy and Mazdak's Revolt," *Studia Iranica*, vol. 11, 1982, pp. 111-122.

Gernet, J. *A History of Chinese Civilization*, Cambridge University Press, 1982.

Gignoux, Ph. & Gyselen, R. *Sceaux sasanides de diverses collections privées*, Éditions Peeters, Leuven, 1982.

_____. *Bulles et sceax sassanides de diverses collections*, Studia Iranica - Cahier 4, Association pour l'avanement des études iraniennes, Paris, 1987.

_____. *Les Quatre inscription du mage Kirdīr*, textes et concordances, Association pour l'avancement des études iraniennes, Leuven, 1991.

_____. "Sāsān ou le dieu protecteur," *Proceedings of the Third European Conference of Iranian Studies*, Part 1: Old and Middle Iranian Studies, ed. N. Sims-Williams, Wiesbaden, 1998, pp. 1-7

_____. *Man and Cosmos in Ancient Iran*, IsIAO, Roma, 2001.

Gnoli, G. *Zoroaster's Time and Homeland*, IsMEO, Napoli, 1980.

122   *Bibliography*

_____. *The Idea of Iran, an Essay on Its Origin*, Serie Orientale Roma LXII, Rome, 1989.

Göbl, R. *Sasanidische Numismatik*, Klinkhardt & Biermann, Braunschweig, 1968.

Greatrex, G. *Rome and Persia at war: 502-532*, Leeds, 1998.

_____ and S.N.C. Lieu, *The Roman Eastern Frontier and the Persian Wars. Part II AD 363-630*, Routledge, London and New York, 2002.

Gunder Frank, A. *ReOrient: Global Economy in the Asian Age*, Berkeley, Los Angeles, London, 1998.

Gurnet, F. "Deux notes à propos du monnayage de Xusrō II," *Revue belge de Numismatique*, 140, 1994, pp. 25-41.

Gyselen, R. *La géographie administrative de l'empire sassanide, les témoignages siglloraphiques*, Centre National pour la Recherce Scientifique et de l'Associaton pour l'Avancement des Etudes Iraniennes, Paris, 1989.

_____. "Note de glyptique sassanide les cachets personnels de l'ohrmazd-mogbed," *Études irano-aryennes offertes á Gilbert Lazard*, ed. C.-H de Fouchécour and Ph. Gignoux, Association pour l'avancement des études iraniennes, Paris, 1989, pp. 185-192.

_____. "Les sceaux des mages de l'Iran sassanide," *Au carrefour des religions Mélanges offerts á Philippe Gignoux*, ed. R. Gyselen, Res Orientales, Vol. VII, Groupe pour l'étude de la civilisation du moyen-orient, Bures-sur-Yvette, 1995, pp. 121-150.

_____. *The Four Generals of the Sasanians Empire: some Sigillographic Evidence*, Roma, 2001.

_____. *New Evidence for Sasanian Numismatics: The Collection of Ahmad Saeedi*, Res Orientalis XVI, Bures-sur-Yvette, 2004.

_____. *Sasanian Seals and Sealings in the A. Saeedi Collection*, Acta Iranica 44, Louvanii, 2007.

Hansen, O. *Die mittelpersischen Papyri der Papyrussammlung der Staatlischen Museen zu Berlin*, Verlag der Akademie der Wissenschaften, Berlin, 1938.

Harmatta, J. "The middle Persian-Chinese Bilingual Inscription from Hsian and the Chinese-Sasanian Relations," *La Persia nel Medioevo*, Accademia Nazionale dei Lincei, Roma, 1971, pp. 363-376.

Harper, P.O. *The Royal Hunter, Art of the Sasanian Empire*, The Asia Society, New York, 1978.

Henning, W.B. "Mani's Last Journey," *Bulletin of the School of Oriental and African Studies*, vol. x, part 4, 1942, pp. 941-953.

_____. "The Inscription of Firuzabad," *Asia Major*, vol. 4, 1954, pp. 98-102.

_____. "Notes on the Great Inscription of Šāpūr I," *Professor Jackson Memorial Volume*, Bombay, 1954, pp. 25-29.

_____. *W.B. Henning – Selected Papers*, Acta Iranica, vols. V and VI, E.J. Brill, Leiden, 1977.

Herrenschmidt, C. *Les Trios écritures: Langue, nombre, code*, Gallimard, 2007.

Herrmann, G. *The Iranian Revival*, Elsevier, Phaidon, 1977.

_____. "Shapur I in the East: Reflections from his Voctory Reliefs," *The Arts and Archaeology of Ancient Persia, New Light on the*

124   *Bibliography*

Parthian and Sasanian Empires, eds. V.S. Curtin, R. Hillenbrand, J.M. Rogers, I.B. Taurus, 1998, pp. 38-51

Herzfeld, E. *Iran in the Ancient East,* Hacker Art Books, New York, reprint 1988.

Hinz, W. *Altiranische Funde und Forschungen,* Walter de Gruyter & Co., Berlin, 1969.

_____. "Mani and Kardēr," *La Persia nel Medievo,* Accademia Nazionale dei Lincei, Roma, 1971, pp. 485-499.

Howard-Johnston, J. "The Two Great Powers in Late Antiquity: a Comparison," *The Byzantine and Early Islamic Near East,* vol. III, ed. A. Cameron, The Darwin Press, Inc., New Jersey, 1995, pp. 157-226.

_____. "Pride and Fall: Khusro II and His Regime, 626-628," *La Persia e bisanzio,* Roma, 2004, pp. 93-114.

Hoyland, R.G. *Arabia and the Arabs, From the Bronze Age to the Coming of Islam,* Routledge, London and New York, 2001.

Huyse, Ph. "Noch einmal zu Parallelen zwischen Achaemeniden- und Sāsānideninschriften," *Archäologische Mitteilungen aus Iran,* vol. 23, 1990, pp. 177-183.

_____. "Kerdīr and the first Sasanians," *Proceedings of the Third European Conference of Iranian Studies,* ed. N. Sims-Williams, Part 1, Dr. Ludwig Reichert Verlag, Wiesbaden, 1998, pp. 109-120.

_____. *Die dreisprachige Inschrift Šābuhrs I. an der Ka'ba-I Zardušt,* 2 vols., Corpus Inscriptionum Iranicarum, London, 2000.

_____. "Die sasanidische Königstitulatur: Eine Gegenüberstellung der Quellen," *Ērān ud Anērān. Studien zu den Beziehungen zwischen dem Sasanidenreich und der Mittelmeerwelt.*

Beiträge des Internationalen Colloquiums in Eutin, 8.-9. Juni 2000, eds. J. Wiesehöfer and Ph. Huyse, München, 2006, pp. 181-202.

Inostrantsev, K. *Motal'ātī darbare-ye Sāsānīān*, BTNK, Tehran, 1348.

De Jong, A. "Sub Specie Maiestatis: Reflections on Sasanian Court Rituals," *Zoroastrian Ritual in Context*, ed. M. Stausberg, Brill, Leiden, 2004, pp. 345-366.

Kettenhofen, E. *Die römisch-persischen Kriege des 3. Jahrhunderts n. Chr. nach der Inscrift Šāpuhrs I. an der Ka'be-ye Zartošt (ŠKZ)*, Dr. Ludwig Reichert Verlag, Wiesbaden, 1982.

_____. *Das Sāsānidenreich*, TAVO, Dr. Ludwig Reichert Verlag, Wiesbaden, 1993.

_____. "Deportations. ii. In the Parthian and Sasanian Periods," *Encyclopaedia Iranica*, Vol. VII, 1996, pp. 297-308.

Kister, M.J. "Al-Hīra, Some notes on its relations with Arabia," *Arabica*, vol. xi, 1967,pp. 143-169.

Kuhrt, A. and S. Sherwin-White, *From Samarkhand to Sardis: A New Approach to the Seleucid Empire*, London, 1993.

Labourt, J. *Le Christianisme dans l'empire perse*, Paris, 1904.

Laufer, B. *Sino-Iranica: Chinese Contributions to the History of Civilization in Ancient Iran, with Special Reference to the History of Cultivated Plants and Products*, Field Museum of Natural History, Publication 201, Anthropological Series, vol. 15, no. 3, Chicago, 1919.

Lieu, S.N.C. "Captives, Refugees, and Exiles: A Study of Cross-Frontier Civilian Movements and Contacts between Rome and Persia from Valerian to Jovian," *The Defense of the Roman and By-*

zantine East, Proceedings of a colloquium held at the University of Sheffield in April 1986, ed. P. Freeman and D. Kennedy, part ii, British Institute of Archaeology at Ankara, Monograph No. 8, BAR International Series 297, 1986, pp. 473-508.

Lincoln, B. *Religion, Empire, and Torture*, Chicago, University of Chicago Press, 2007.

Lukonin, V.G. "Administrative division of Parthian and Sasanian Period," *The Cambridge History of Iran*, ed. E. Yarshater, Cambridge University Press, Cambridge, 1983, pp. 681-746.

_____. *Tamddun-e Irān-e Sāsānī*, Translated from Russian into Persian by I. Ridā, Scientific & Cultural Publication Company, Tehran, 1987.

MacKenzie, "Shapur's Shooting," *The Bulletin of the School of Oriental and Africa Studies*, Vol. 41, 1978, pp. 499-511.

_____. "Mani's Šābuhragān I," *Bulletin of the School of Oriental and African Studies*, 1979, pp. 288-310.

_____. "Mani's Šābuhragān II," *Bulletin of the School of Oriental and African Studies*, 1979, pp. 500-534.

_____. *The Sasanian Rock Reliefs at Naqsh-i Rustam*, Iranische Denkmäler, 1989.

Macuch, M. "Sasanidische Institutionen in früh-Islamischer Zeit," *Transition Periods in Iranian History*, L'Association pour l'avancement de études iraniennes, Paris, 1987, pp. 178-179.

_____. "Charitable Foundations. i. In the Sasanian Period," *Encyclopaedia Iranica*, 1991, pp. 380-382.

Malek, H.M. "The Coinage of the Sasanian King Kavād II (AD 628)," *The Numismatic Chronicle*, vol. 155, 1995, pp. 119-129

_____. & Sarkhosh Curtis, V. "History and Coinage of the Sasanian Queen Bōrān (AD 629-631)," *The Numismatic Chronicle*, vol. 158, 1998, p. 113-129.

Marquart, J. *Ērānšahr nach der Geographie des Ps. Moses Xorenac'i*, Weidmannsche Buchhandlung, Berlin, 1901.

Maškūr, M.J. *Tārīkh-e Sīyāsī Sasaniān*, Tehran, 1366

Melikian-Chirvani, A.S. "The Iranian bazm in Early Persian Sources," *Banquets d'Orient*, ed. R. Gyselen, Res Orientales IV, Bures-sur-Yvette, 1992, pp. 95-120.

Mochiri, M.I. *Études de numismatique Iranienne sous les Sassanides*, Tome I, Téhéran, 1972.

_____. *Études de numismatique Iranienne sous les Sassanides*, Tome I, Téhéran, 1982.

Mori, S. "The narrative structure of the Paikuli Inscription," *Orient*, vol. 30-31, 1995, pp. 182-193.

Morony, M.G. "Continuity and Change in the Administrative Geography of Late Sasanian and Early Islamic al-'Iraq," *IRAN, Journal of the British Institute of Persian Studies*, vol. XX, 1982, pp. 1-49.

_____. *Iraq After the Muslim Conquest*, Princeton University Press, Princeton, New Jersey, 1984.

_____. "Syria Under the Persians 610-629," *Proceedings of the Second Symposium on the History of Bilād al-Shām During the Early Islamic Period up to 40 A.H. / 640 A.D.*, ed. M.A. Bakhit, Amman, 1987, pp. 87-95.

_____. "Mazdak," *The Encylcopaedia of Islam*, vol. vi, 1991, pp. 449-452.

128   *Bibliography*

_____. "Sāsānids," *The Encycleopaedia of Islam*, 1998, pp. 70-83.

_____. "Population Transfers between Sasanian Iran and the Byzantine Empire," *La Persia e bisanzio*, Roma, 2004, pp. 161-180.

Nafisī, S. *Tārīkh-e tamaddun-e Irān-e Sāsānī*, Tehran, 1331.
Nai, H. *Studies in Chinese Archaeology*, The Institute of Archaeological Academia Sinica, Peking, 1961.

Neusner, J. "How Much Iranian in Jewish Babylonia?," *Journal of the American Oriental Society*, vol. 95, no. 2, 1975, pp. 184-190.

_____. "Jews in Iran," *The Cambridge History of Iran*, vol. 3(2), ed. E. Yarshater, Cambridge University Press, 1983, p. 909-923.

Nititin, A.B. "Middle Persian Ostraca from South Turkmenistan," *East and West*, vol. 42, no. 1, 1992, pp. 105-121.

Omrānī, N. *Šāpuragān*, Aštād Publishers, Tehran, 1379.

Panaino, A. *La novella degli scacchi e della tavola reale. Un'antica fonte orientale sui due giochi da tavola piu diffuse nel mondo eurasiatico tra Tardoantico e Medioevo e sulla loro simbologia militare e astrologica*, Mimesis, Milan, 1999.

_____. "The baγān of the Fratarakas: Gods or 'divine' Kings?," *Religious themes and texts of pre-Islamic Iran and Central Asia: Studies in honour of Professor Gherardo Gnoli on the occasion of his 65th birthday on 6 December 2002*, eds. C. Cereti, M. Maggi, E. Provasi, Wiesbaden, 2002, pp. 283-306.

_____. "Astral Characters of Kingship in the Sasanian and Byzantine World," *La Persia e Bisanzio*, Accademia Nazionale dei Lincei, Roma, 2004, pp. 555-594.

Peters, F.E. *The Harvest of Hellenism, A History of the Near East from Alexander the Great to the Triumph of Christianity*, Barnes and Noble, New York, 1970 (reprint 1996).

Piacentini, V.F. "Ardashīr I Pāpakān and the wars against the Arabs: Working hypothesis on the Sasanian hold on the Gulf," *Proceedings of the Seminar for Arabian Studies*, Vol. 15, London, 1985, pp. 57-78.

Pigulevskaïa, N.V. *Les villes de l'état iranien aux époques parthe et sassanide*, Paris, 1963.

Pirart, E. *Kayān Yasn, l'origine avestique des dynasties mythiques d'Iran*, Barcelona, Editorial Ausa, 1992.

Piras, A. "Mesopotamian Sacred Marriage and Pre-Islamic Iran," *Melammu Symposia IV*, eds. A. Panaino and A. Piras, Milano, 2004, pp. 249-259.

Pourshariati, P. *Decline and Fall of the Sasanian Empire: The Sasanian-Parthian Confederacy and the Arab Conquest of Iran*, IB Tauris, (forthcoming 2008).

Rawlinson, G. *The Seventh Great Oriental Monarchy or the Geography, History and Antiquities of the Sassanian or new Persian Empire*, Dodd, mead & Company, New York, 1875.

Rose, J. "Three Queens, Two Wives, and a Goddess: Roles and Images of Women in Sasanian Iran," *Women in the Medieval Islamic World*, ed. G. Hambly, 1998, pp. 29-54.

Rubin, Z. "The Reforms of Khusrō Anūshirwān," in *The Byzantine and Early Islamic Near East, States, Resources and Armies*, vol. III, ed. A. Cameron, Princeton, 1995, pp. 227-296.

_____. "The Roman Empire in the Res Gestae Divi Saporis," *Ancient Iran and theMediterranean World*, ed. E. Dābrowa, Electrum 2, Jagiellonian University Press, Kraków, 1998, pp. 177-185.

Russell, J.R. "Advocacy of the Poor: The Maligned Sasanian Order," *Journal of the K. R. Cama Oriental Institute*, Bombay, 1986, p. 136

_____. *Zoroastrianism in Armenia*, Harvard Iranian Series, Cambridge, Massachusetts, 1987.

_____. "Kartīr and Mānī: a shamanistic model of their conflict," *Iranica Varia: Papers in honor of Professor Ehsan Yarshater*, E.J. Brill, Leiden, 1990, pp. 180-193.

Sarkārāti, B. "Akhbār-e Tārīkhī dar Āthār ī Mānavī: Mānī wa Šāpūr," *Sāyehā-ye Šekār Šode*, Našr Qatre, Tehran, 1378, pp. 163-192.

Sarkhosh Curtis, V. and Malek, H.M. "History and Coinage of the Sasanian Queen Bārān (AD 629-631)," *The Numismatic Chronicle*, vol. 158, 1998, p. 113-129.

Schafer, E.H. "Iranian Merchants in T'and Dynasty Tales," *University of California Publications in Semitic Philology*, vol. 11, 1951, pp. 403-422.

_____. *The Golden Peaches of Samarkand, A Study of T'ang Exotics*, University of California Press, 1963.

Schwartz. M. "*Sasm, Sesen, St. Sisinnios, Sesengen Barpharangès, and ... 'Semanglof,'" *Bulletin of the Asia Institute*, vol. 10, 1996, pp. 253-257.

_____. "Sesen: a Durable East Mediterranean God in Iran," *Proceedings of the Third European Conference of Iranian Studies held in Cambridge, 11th to 15th September 1995*, Part 1, Old and Middle Iranian Studies, ed. N. Sims-Williams, Wiesbaden, 1998, Dr. Ludwig Reichert Verlag, pp. 9-13.

Shahbazi, A.Sh. "Narse's Relief at Naqš-i Rustam," *Archäologische Mitteilungen aus Iran*, vol. 16, 1983, pp. 255-268.

_____. "Army," *Encyclopaedia Iranica*, Vol. II, 1987, pp. 489-499.

_____. "Studies in Sasanian Prosopography: III Barm-i Dilak: Symbolism of Offering Flowers," *The Art and Archaeology of Ancient Persia*, ed. V. Sarkhosh, et. al., I.B. Tauris, London, 1998, pp. 58-66.

_____. "Early Sasanians' Claim to Achaemenid Heritage," *Nāme-ye Irān-e Bāstān, The International Journal of Ancient Iranian Studies*, vol. 1, no. 1, 2001, pp. 61-74.

_____. "Ardašīr II," *Encyclopaedia Iranica*, ed. E. Yarshater (http://www.iranica.com/newsite/).

_____. "Hormozd II," *Encyclopaedia Iranica*, ed. E. Yarshater, (http://www.iranica.com/newsite/).

_____. "Hormozd III," *Encyclopaedia Iranica*, ed. E. Yarshater, (http://www.iranica.com/newsite/).

_____. "Hormozd IV," *Encyclopaedia Iranica*, ed. E. Yarshater, (http://www.iranica.com/newsite/).

_____. "Sasanian" *Encyclopaedia Iranica*, ed. E. Yarshater, 2005 (http://www.iranica.com/newsite/).

Shaked, Sh. *Dualism in Transformation: Varieties of Religion in Sasanian Iran*, Jordan Lectures in Comparative Religion, School of Oriental and African Studies, University of London, 1994.

Sivan, H. "Palestine between Byzantium and Persia (CE 614-618)," *La Persia e bisanzio*, Roma, 2004, pp. 77-92.

Shaki, M. "The Social Doctrine of Mazdak in the Light of Middle Persian Evidence," *Archív Orientálni*, vol. 46, 1978, pp. 289-306.

_____. "The Dēnkard Account of the History of the Zoroastrian Scriptures," *Archív Orientálni*, vol. 49, 1981, p. 119-138.

_____. "Drist-Dēnān," *Ma'ārif*, vol. 10, no. 1, 1372, pp. 28-52.

_____. "The Cosmological and Cosmological Teachings of Mazdak," *Papers in Honour of Professor Mary Boyce*, Acta Iranica 25, E.J. Brill, Leiden, 1985, pp. 527-543.

_____. "Sasan ke bud?," *Iranshenasi*, vol. 2, no. 1, Spring 1990, pp. 78-80.

Shayegan, M.R. "The Evolution of the Concept of Xwadāy 'God'," *Acta Orientalia Academiae Scientiarum Hungaricae*, Vol. 51, Nos. 1-2, 1998, pp. 31-54.

_____. "Hormozd I," *Encycelopaedia Iranica*, ed. E. Yarshater, (http://www.iranica.com/newsite/).

Sims-Williams, N. "The Sogdian Fragment of Leningrad II: Mani at the Court of the Shahanshah," *Bulletin of the Asia Institute*, vol. 4, 1990, pp. 281-288.

Skjærvø, P.O. and H. Humbach, *The Sassanian Inscription of Paikuli*, Wiesbaden, 1983.

_____. "Kirdir's Vision: Translation and Analysis," *Archaeologische Mitteilungen aus Iran*, vol. 16, 1983, pp. 269-306.

_____. "Thematic and linguistic parallels in the Achaemenian and Sassanian inscriptions," *Papers in Honour of Professor Mary Boyce*, Acta Iranica 25, E.J. Brill, Leiden, 1985, pp. 593-603.

_____. "The Joy of the Cup: A Pre-Sasanian Middle Persian Inscription on a Silver Bowl," *Bulletin of the Asia Institute*, vol. 11, 1997, pp. 93-104.

Soudavar, A. *The Aura of the Kings: Legitimacy and Divine Sanction in Iranian Kingship*, Mazda Publishers, Costa Mesa, 2003.

Le Strange, G. *The Lands of the Eastern Caliphate*, Barnes and Noble, New York, 1966.

Stratos, A.N. *Byzantium in the Seventh Century*, Vol. I, Amsterdam, 1968.

Tafazzolī, A. "A List of Trades and Crafts in the Sassanian Period," *Archaeologische Mitteilungen aus Iran*, vol. 7, 1974, pp. 191-196.

_____. "Un chapitre du Dēnkard sur les guerriers," *Au carrefour des religions: Mélanges offerts á Philippe Gignoux*, Res Orientales VII, Peeters, Leuven, 1995, pp. 297-302.

_____. *Sasanian Society*, Ehsan Yarshater Distinguished Lecture Series, Bibliotheca Persica Press, New York, 2000.

Venetis, E. "The Sassanid Occupation of Egypt (7th Cent. A.D) According to Some Pahlavi Papyri Abstracts," *Greco-Arabica*, vols. 9-10, 2004, pp. 403-412.

Walker, J.Th. "The Limits of Late Antiquity: Philosophy between Rome and Iran," *Ancient World*, vol. 33, 2002, pp. 45-69.

_____. *The Legacy of Mesopotamia in Late Antique Iraq: The Legend of Mar Qardagh the Assyrian*, Berkeley and Los Angeles, 2007.

Weber, D. "Ein bisher unbekannter Titel aus spätsassanidischer Zeit?," *Corolla Iranica. Paperes in honour of Prof. D.N. MacKenzie on the occasion of his 65th birthday*, Frankfurt, 1991, pp. 228-235.

134   *Bibliography*

_____. *Ostraca, Papyri und Pergamente*, Corpus Inscriptionum Iranicarum, Part III Pahlavi Inscriptions, London, 1992.

Widengren, G. "The Establishment of the Sasanian dynasty in the light of new evidence," *La Persia nel Medioevo*, Academia Nazionale dei Lincei, Roma, 1971, pp. 711-782.

Wiesehöfer, J. "Ardašīr I," Encyclopaedia Iranica, ed. E. Yarshater, vol. II, 1987, pp. 371-376.

_____. *Die "Dunklen Jahrhunderte" der Persis. Untersuchungen zur Geschichte und Kultur von Fārs in frühhellenistischer Zeit (330-140 v. Chr.)*, Munich, 1994.

_____. *Ancient Persia From 550 BC to 650 AD*, I.B. Tauris Publishers, London & New York, 1996, pp. 151-222.

_____. "Fārs II. – History in the Pre-Islamic Period," *Encycelopaedia Iranica*, ed. E. Yarshater, vol. IX, New York, 1999, pp. 333-337.

_____. *Iraniens, Grecs et Romains*, Studia Iranica, Cahier 32, Paris, 2005.

_____. "Statt einer Einleitung: 'Randkultur' oder 'Nabel der Welt'? Das Sasanidenreich und der Westen. Anmerkungen eines Althistorikers," *Ērān ud Anērān. Studien zu den Beziehungen zwischen dem Sasanidenreich und der Mittelmeerwelt. Beiträge des Internationalen Colloquiums in Eutin, 8.-9. Juni 2000*, eds. J. Wiesehöfer and Ph. Huyse, München, 2006, pp. 9-28.

_____. "Fars under Seleucid and Parthian Rule," The Idea of Iran, The Age of the Parthians, eds. V. Sarkhosh Curtis and S. Stewart, vol. 2, London, 2007, pp. 37-49.

Wolf, E. *Europe and the People Without History*, Berkeley and Los Angeles, 1982.

Yarshater, E. "Mazdakism," *The Cambridge History of Iran*, vol. III (2), Cambridge, Massachusetts, 1983, pp. 991-1024.

Zaehner, R.C. *Zurvan, A Zoroastrian Dilemma*, Biblio and Tannen, New York, 1955 (reprint 1972).

Zakeri, M. Sāsānid Soldiers in Early Muslilm Society. The Origins of 'Ayyārān and Futuwwa, Wiesbaden, 1995.

Zarrīnkūb, R. *Tārīkh-e Sīyāsī-ye Sāsānīān*, Tehran, 1379 (reprint 1381).

Index